The Civil Procedure Rules:

Fast Track Personal Injury Claims

Part of the
Personal Injury
Service from CLT and Barnard's Inn Chambers

The Civil Procedure Rules:

Fast Track Personal Injury Claims

The Civil Procedure Rules

Fast Track Personal Injury Claims

by
Matthew Chapman

LLB (Hons), LLM
Barrister
Barnard's Inn Chambers, London

CLT Professional Publishing
A Division of Central Law Training Ltd

© The Author and CLT Professional Publishing 1999

Published by
CLT Professional Publishing Ltd
(A division of Central Law Group)
31–33 Stonehills House
Howardsgate
Welwyn Garden City
AL8 6PU

ISBN 1 85811 226 5

Typeset by Jane Conway

Printed and bound in Great Britain by
MPG Books Ltd, Bodmin, Cornwall

Table of Contents

Preface   *ix*
Table of Statutes and Rules   *xi*
Table of Cases   *xiv*

1   Introduction   1
     The ancien regime and procedural flexibility   1
     Revolution: The Woolf Report   3
     The Response to reform   6

2   The Fast Track Rules: Transitional Arrangements
     and General Features   8
     The Scheme of the Rules: Commencement and
          Uniformity   8
     The Fast Track: principal characteristics   10

3   Getting Started: Pre-Action Protocol and Commencing
     Proceedings   11
     Pre-action protocol for personal injury claims   11
     Commencing proceedings   13
     Statements of case   13
     The parties   14
     The Claim Form and particulars of claim: content
          and time limits   15
     The Defence: content and time limits   17
     Third party claims   19
     Further information   19

4   Allocation to the Fast Track   20
     General Features   20
     The questionnaire   20
     Stay of proceedings for alternative dispute resolution   22
     The appropriate track   22

5   Fast Track Directions   24
        General Features   24
        Allocation directions   25
        Disclosure   25
        Inspection   26
        Further directions   26
        Varying the directions order   28
        Failure to comply with directions   28

6   Applications, Summary Disposal and Summary Judgment   30
        Applications and interim remedies   30
        Part 23 formalities   30
        The range of interim remedies   31
        Interim payments   32
        Summary disposal   33
        Summary judgment   34

7   Evidence: Lay Witnesses and Experts   36
        Lay Witnesses: general features   36
        The form of the witness statement   37
        Experts: general features   38
        The single joint expert   39
        The form of the expert report   39
        Assessors   40

8   Offers to Settle and Payments into Court   41
        General features   41
        Form and content   41
        Time limits   43
        Consequences of a Part 36 offer or payment   44

9   The Fast Track Trial   45
        General features   45
        The listing questionnaire   46
        Postponing the trial   46
        Pre-trial document preparation: trial bundles   47
        The hearing   48

10 Costs   51
    General features   51
    The key principles and definitions   52
    A duty to inform the absent client   52
    Fast track fixed costs   53
    Fast track pre-trial costs: the court's discretion as to costs   53
    Discretion as to costs: the conduct of the parties   54
    Discretion as to costs: Part 36 offers and payments   54
    Fast track pre-trial costs: the range of costs orders
        available to the Court   56
    Fast track pre-trial costs: the standard and indemnity
        basis for assessment of costs   56
    Fast track trial costs: the method of assessment   58
    Fast track trial costs: the fixed sums   60
    The procedure for assessing costs   61
    The assessment of conditional fee arrangements   62
    Wasted costs   63

    Index   65

Preface

"Before sea or land, before even sky
Which contains all,
Nature wore only one mask –
Since called Chaos.
A huge agglomeration of upset."

Ted Hughes, "Creation" from *Tales from Ovid* (Faber, 1997)

"In the Beginning the light And the first hour
when lips still in clay
try out the things of the world"

Odysseus Elytis, "Genesis" from *The Axion Esti* (Anvil, Selected Poems, 1981 – translated by E Keeley and G Savidis)

On 23 April 1999 the County Courts in England and Wales closed. When they reopened on 26 April 1999 a huge change in the manner in which all civil cases are litigated had taken place. On that date the Civil Procedure Rules came into force. While it would be exaggeration to claim that 26 April 1999 saw chaos replaced by order, no civil practitioner can afford to underestimate the scale and significance of the change that is now happening.

As the Introduction to this book indicates, the reforms that are now codified by the Rules were preceded by a good deal of Judge led case law. If the Woolf reforms can be called a revolution then they are a Judge driven common law revolution. It is clear from cases like *Beachley Property Ltd* v *Edgar* [1997] PNLR 197 CA, *The Mortgage Corporation* v *Sandoes* [1997] PNLR 263 CA and, more recently, *Bannister* v *SGB Plc* [1998] 1 WLR 1123 CA that the Court of Appeal has, for some time, been an active advocate for change. It is in the expression of discontent with the old system, which is robustly articulated in these and other cases, that the seeds of reform can be found.

The Rules place an overriding objective at their centre. The overriding objective directs the Court to deal with cases justly and justice apparently demands equality, cost-effectiveness, proportionality, speed and the efficient allocation of Court resources (CPR 1.1). Perhaps, the greatest innovation in the Rules is the Courts' new power of case management in order to ensure that the overriding objective is achieved (CPR 1.4). From 26 April 1999 the Court, rather than the parties, is in the driving seat in the management of litigation and the Court's power to manage extends from commencement to trial, embracing all the interlocutory stages of proceedings. It is primarily with this aspect of the change, and the manner in which it impacts on personal injury claims of modest value, that this book is concerned. It is sometimes easier to define what something is not than precisely to spell out what it is. This book is not intended to be a comprehensive guide to the fast track and personal injury Parts of the Rules, much less an exhaustive commentary on each relevant, or potentially relevant, Rule. Instead, this book aims to provide an accessible and succinct guide to those Parts of the Rules that the personal injury practitioner will commonly encounter while steering a case down the fast track to settlement or trial. In time the task of predicting how the Rules will be applied will become clearer, but, for the time being, we are all going to have to learn to try out the things of Lord Woolf's new world. Any errors in the material that follows are mine alone.

Matthew Chapman
Barnard's Inn Chambers, Holborn, London.
Maundy Thursday, 1999.

Table of Statutes and Rules

Civil Procedure Rules, ...3, 8
1
    1.1, ...x
    1.4, ...x
3
    3.3, ...34
    3.4(2), ...33
    3.9(1)(e), ...28
    PD, ...34
7, ...13
    7.1, ...13
    7.2, ...15
    7.4(1), ...16
    7.4(2), ...16
    7.4(3), ...16
    7.5, ...16
    7.6(2), ...16
    7.6(3), ...16
    7.6(3)(c), ...16
    7.6(4), ...16
    7.8(1), ...16
    PD, ...13
14
    14.5, ...21
15
    15.10, ...21
    15.4, ...18
    15.5, ...18
    15.9, ...18
16
    16.2(1), ...15
    16.5(1), ...17
    16.5(2), ...17
    16.5(3), ...17

16.5(5), ...17
16.5(6), ...18
16.6–16.7, ...18
PD 16, 17, 18
17, ...31
18, ...19, 31
    18.1, ...19
    PD, ...19
19, ...14, 15, 31
    19.1(2), ...14
    19.1(3), ...14
    19.1(4), ...14
    19.4(2), ...15
    19.4(3), ...15
    19.4(4)(a), ...15
    19.4(4)(b), ...15
20, ...19
    20.13(2), ...19
    20.4(1)–(2), ...18
21
    21.1(2), ...14
    21.1, ...14
22, ...31, 36, 37, 40
    22.2(1), ...13
    22.2(2), ...13
    PD, ...13
23, ...30, 43
    23.3(1), ...30
    23.6, ...30, 31
    23.7(1)(b), ...31
    23.7(2)–(3), ...30
    PD, ...30, 31
24, ...30, 31, 34
    24.1, ...34

24.2, ...35
24.4(1), ...34
PD, ...35
25, ...30, 31–2
25.6(1), ...32
25.6(3), ...32
25.6(4), ...32
25.6(5), ...32
25.7(1), ...32–33
25.7(2), ...33
25.7(4)–(5), ...33
26, ...20
26.3(1), ...20
26.3(2), ...21
26.3(6), ...20
26.4(1), ...20, 22
26.4(2), ...22
26.4(3), ...22
26.4(5), ...22
26.5, ...20
26.5(3), ...23
26.5(5), ...21
26.6(1), ...22
26.6(4), ...20, 22
26.6(5), ...20
26.6(5)(a), ...22
26.6(5)(b), ...22
26.7, ...22
26.8(1), ...23
26.8(2), ...22
PD, ...21, 23, 48, 49, 59
28, ...24, 25
28.2(1)–(2), ...24
28.2 (2)(a), ...8
28.3(1), ...24
28.2(4), ...24
28.5, ...24
28.5(2), ...46
28.5(3), ...46
28.6, ...46

28.6(1), ...27
28.6(2), ...27, 46
28.7, ...48
PD, ...24, 25, 26, 27, 28,
.........29, 37, 46, 47, 50
31
31.3(1), ...26
31.3(2), ...26
31.5(1), ...25
31.6, ...25
31.8, ...26
31.10(5), ...25
31.10(7), ...26
31.12, ...26
31.14, ...26
31.16, ...26
31.17, ...26
31.19, ...26
PD, ...26
32, ...36
32.1(1), ...36
32.1(2)–(3), ...36, 49
32.2, ...36, 47
32.5(1), ...36
32.5(2)–(4), ...49
32.6(1), ...36
32.6(2), ...36
32.9, ...36
32.10, ...37
32.14, ...14
PD, ...37
33, ...36
33.6, ...48
35, ...38
35.1, ...38
35.3, ...38
35.4(1)–(2), ...38
35.5(1), ...39
35.5(2), ...38
35.6, ...39

35.7(1), ...39
35.7(3), ...39
35.8(1)–(2), ...39
35.8(5), ...39
35.14(1), ...38
35.14(2)–(3), ...38
35.15, ...40
35.15(4), ...40
35.15(5)–(6), ...40
PD, ...39, 40
36,.............41, 42, 43, 44, 55
36.1(2), ...41
36.5(1)–(3), ...42
36.5(6), ...43
36.6(1)–(2), ...42
36.6(3)–(4), ...42
36.7, ...42
36.7(2), ...42
36.7(3), ...42
36.8(1), ...43
36.8(2), ...43
36.8(5), ...43
36.9(1), ...42
36.9(2), ...42
36.10(1), ...42
36.10(2), ...42
36.10(2)(c), ...42
36.11(1), ...43
36.12(1), ...43
36.13, ...55
36.13(2), ...55
36.14, ...55
36.15(1), ...44
36.15(3)(a), ...44
36.15(3)(b), ...44
36.19(1)–(2), ...44
36.20, ...55
36.21(2), ...55
36.21(3), ...55
36.21(4), ...56

36.21(5), ...56
PD, ...42, 43
39
39.5(1), ...47
39.5(2), ...47
PD, ...48
43, ...51
44, ...51, 55
44.2, ...53
44.3(1), ...53
44.3(2)(a), ...52
44.3(2)(b), ...52
44.3(4)(a), ...54, 55
44.3(4)(b), ...54
44.3(4)(c), ...41, 55
44.3(5)(a), ...54
44.3(5)(b), ...54
44.3(6), ...56
44.4(1), ...56
44.4(2)(a), ...57
44.4(2)(b), ...57
44.4(3), ...57
44.7, ...61
44.9, ...58
44.9(2), ...58
44.10(1), ...58
44.10(2), ...58
44.11(2), ...58
44.13(1), ...52
PD, ...53, 57, 61, 62
45, ...51
46, ...51, 58
46.1(2)(3)(a), ...59
46.1(2)(3)(b), ...59
46.2, ...59
46.2(1), ...60
46.2(2), ...60
46.3(2), ...60
46.3(3)–(4), ...60
46.3(6), ...59

46.3(7)–(8), ...60
46.4(1), ...60
46.4(3), ...61
46.4(4), ...61
PD, ...59
47, ...51, 62
48, ...51
48.7, ...63
PD, ...62–63
51
PD, ...8, 9
Protocol,
Annex B, ...11–13, 54
Schedule 2, ...9

County Courts Act 1984
Section 51, ...17
Section 52, ...32
Section 53, ...32
County Court Rules
Order 17, rule 11, ...1, 10, 46
Order 19, rule 4(2)(c), ...7

Limitation Act 1980, 15

Rules of the Supreme Court
Order 36, rules 1–9, ...4
Supreme Court Act 1981, ...17

Table of Cases

Bank of England v Vagliano Brothers [1891]
AC 107 (HL(E)), ...9
Bannister v SGB Plc [1998] 1 WLR 1123 CA, ...ix, 1, 2
Beachley Properties Ltd v Edgar [1997] PNLR 197 CA, ...ix, 2

Hytec Information Systems Limited v Coventry City
Council (1996) *The Times* 31 December, ...33

The Mortgage Corporation v Sandoes [1997]
PNLR 263 CA, ...ix, 2, 28, 37, 47

Chapter 1

Introduction

"*We certainly cannot go on as we are.*"

Bannister v *SGB Plc* [1998] 1 WLR 1123, 1163 *per* Saville LJ CA

"*The fast track depends ... on a change of culture throughout the system which will be supported by the new rules which I am drafting. It will affect judges and court staff as well as the profession. The new system will depend very much on good and clear forms, notes for guidance and practice guides, changes in the listing practices, and appropriate information technology in both courts and solicitors'offices to ensure that the requirements of the timetable are properly diarised.*"

Lord Woolf MR, *Access to Justice* (Final Report, July 1996), section II, chapter 2, paragraph 38

The ancien regime and procedural flexibility

The dominant characteristic of the former system of civil justice, as it applied to cases of modest value, was procedural flexibility. For the typical personal injury claim, litigated in the County Court, the road to trial was commonly littered with consent orders for the extension of procedural time-limits and strewn with repeat directions orders. While the advent of automatic directions under CCR Order 17, rule 11, and its accompanying timetable, constituted an attempt to impose some order on procedural chaos the experience of this writer was that the timetable was generally treated only as a target and that parties were actively encouraged by the courts to set their own time-limits.

In spite of procedural flexibility at District Judge level the Court of Appeal, from time to time, became impatient with the failure of some litigants to observe the time-limits prescribed by the County Court

Rules and by directions orders. *Beachley Property Ltd* v *Edgar* [1997] PNLR 197 CA, represented something of a high water mark when it came to judicial activism in this area of the law. However, the tide subsequently receded and, in *The Mortgage Corporation* v *Sandoes* [1997] PNLR 263 CA, the Court of Appeal, while emphasizing that the time-limits in the County Court Rules, and in directions orders, were rules to be observed and not merely targets to be attempted, also gave at least implicit sanction to the view that extensions of time would generally be granted, unless the same resulted in the vacation or adjournment of the trial date.

Increasingly, the twilight years of the old County Court Rules were accompanied by judicial interventions of this kind as the courts sought to annotate and interpret provisions that had, first, led to confusion and had then formed the subject of *"satellite"* litigation. A good example is provided by *Bannister* v *SGB Plc* [1998] 1 WLR 1123 CA, in which the Court of Appeal heard 19 applications and appeals concerned with the automatic directions regime. A number of the issues raised by the conjoined appeals in *Bannister* turned on the proper *"trigger date"* for the calculation of the all-important *"guillotine date"*, for automatic striking out, 15 months later. If the Court of Appeal's motive was to introduce greater certainty into this process then the means by which it sought to achieve this can be questioned. One example will suffice. The Court, faced with the question when the trigger date should start for cases transferred from the High Court to the County Court, had to choose between the date of order of transfer and the date of receipt of the papers in the County Court. The Court of Appeal chose the former option: the High Court retained jurisdiction until the case, *in a physical sense*, reached the County Court offices. It is surely a dubious proposition that more certainty is created if the date that papers are plucked from a County Court office post-tray is adopted as a trigger date in place of the date that a Judge initials his order on the papers.

Bannister represents, to-date, the Court of Appeal's most ambitious doodle round the edge of the civil justice rules. Appropriately, it concludes with an emphatic call for reform:

> It will be apparent from this judgment that the ill-thought out introduction of an automatic strike-out sanction has caused very great difficulties for many who are involved in the conduct of county court litigation. Many courts are now departing entirely from the automatic strike-out approach to the management of litigation by fixing a date for

the trial at an early stage in appropriate cases. This means that these courts have taken it upon themselves in effect not to leave the fixing of a date to the Plaintiff and to take a proactive role in managing the action. This is of course the approach advocated by Lord Woolf MR in his proposed reforms of the civil justice system ... . In our judgment this alternative approach, reinforced by the much tougher approach of the courts to pardoning delays in the run-up to the date fixed for trial, has a very great deal to commend it.

Revolution: the Woolf Report

It was against this background of confusion and satellite litigation that the Civil Procedure Rules 1998 (SI 1998/3132) (hereafter, *"the Rules"*) were being drafted. The genesis of the Rules can be found in the Reports promulgated by Lord Woolf (assisted by a Committee of Inquiry and a number of specialist working groups). The final draft of Lord Woolf's report on *Access to Justice* (Final Report, July 1996) (hereafter, *"the Woolf Report"*) commenced by identifying defects in the former system of civil justice and by setting out the principles that underpin the reform proposals in the body of the Report.

The defects identified in the old system were, variously, that:

- it was too expensive – the costs often exceeded the value of the claim;
- it was too slow and too unequal – economic inequalities in the relative strengths of the parties was often manifested in procedural unfairness to the weaker party;
- it was too uncertain and was difficult to understand – parties found it difficult to predict the outcome of litigation and found it difficult to understand the manner in which the merits of their case were assessed;
- it was too fragmented – no one had overall responsibility for the administration of civil justice;
- it was too adversarial – cases were run by the parties, rather than by the judge, and the rules of court were either ignored or were not enforced.

(Final Report, Overview, paragraph 2)

The principles for reform, set out in the Woolf Report, were as follows. The new system should:

(a) "be just in the results it delivers;
(b) be fair in the way it treats litigants;
(c) offer appropriate procedures at a reasonable cost;
(d) deal with cases with reasonable speed;
(e) be understandable to those who use it;
(f) be responsive to the needs of those who use it;
(g) provide as much certainty as the nature of particular cases allows; and
(h) be effective: adequately resourced and organized."

(Final Report, Overview, paragraph 1)

While various defects in the former system were identified by the Woolf Report, and a similar number of principles for reform were prescribed, it is clear that the *primary* deficiency identified in the former system was the fact that the interpretation of the Rules of Court and, more particularly, the manner of compliance with them, were often left in the hands of the parties. The chief remedy prescribed by the Report was a fundamental shift from case management by the parties to case management by the judiciary. It was this overriding objective that informed the entire reform process and which now finds expression in the Rules.

Lord Woolf did not have to look far to locate precedents for the kind of hands-on case management that his Report recommends for the entire civil justice system. If case management proves to be a panacea for the various ills of the former system then it is by no means a new phenomenon. The Commercial Court and Official Referee's sub-divisions of the Queen's Bench Division of the High Court have long exercised a jurisdiction to manage closely their own interlocutory business. In the Official Referee's Court, for example, the same Judge is commonly charged with management of all of the interlocutory stages on the way to trial and, upon a case being allocated to him and a summons for directions being heard, is empowered to issue common form directions dealing with all the steps up to and including the fixing of a trial date (see, RSC Ord 36, r 1–9, and commentary thereon).

One of the key proposals in the Woolf Report was the introduction of a tri-partite allocation and timetabling scheme for the case management of all defended cases. The three timetables are referred to in the Report (and in the Civil Procedure Rules) as *"tracks"*. The small claims jurisdiction under the former system has been expanded and made subject to expedited timetabling arrangements. Cases of modest value and little complexity are dealt with under a fast track scheme with a limited procedure, a fixed timetable and fixed costs. The remainder (that is, those cases of higher value and greater complexity) are to be dealt with by means of a multi-track system with individual hands-on management by the judiciary or, where appropriate, by either standard or bespoke directions.

Fast Track

It is worth setting out the general features of the *"new landscape"* envisaged by Lord Woolf for the reformed fast track:

"The timescale of litigation will be shorter and more certain.

(a) All cases will progress to trial in accordance with a timetable set and monitored by the court.
(b) For fast track cases there will be fixed timetables of no more than 30 weeks.
(c) The court will apply strict sanctions to parties who do not comply with the procedures or timetables.
(d) Appeals from case management decisions will be kept to the minimum, and will be dealt with expeditiously.
(e) The court will determine the length of the trial and what is to happen at the trial.

The cost of litigation will be more affordable, more predictable, and more proportionate to the value and complexity of individual cases.

(a) There will be fixed costs for cases on the fast track..."

(Final Report, Overview, paragraph 9)

The response to reform

The Woolf Report recommended that the fast track be used for the vast majority of cases with a claim valued at less than £10,000. The Report describes the consultation process that preceded this proposal. During consultation the Bar Council, in its response, suggested that cases should be allocated to the fast track either by given case type or by choice of the parties themselves, rather than by the monetary value of the claim. The Woolf Report's rejection of these suggestions, and the adoption of financial value as the principal determinant of allocation, was prompted by two considerations. The first was that an automatic jurisdictional limit would inject certainty for litigants and their advisors into the manner in which cases are allocated. Secondly, it was felt that a *prima facie* assumption that a case under £10,000 would be dealt with by the fast track would have the effect of pre-empting potentially lengthy, and costly, disputes between the parties about the proper manner in which a case should be managed (see, Final Report, Chapter 2, Fast Track: General, paragraph 18).

The Woolf Report is preoccupied by the concept of proportionality which is explained in the following terms:

> "Rule 1 of the new rules ... requires the court to deal with cases in ways proportionate to the amount involved, the importance or complexity of the issues, and the parties' financial position. Proportionality underlies the whole concept of the fast track."

> (Final Report, Chapter 2, Fast Track: General, paragraph 19)

The Report rehearses in some detail the arguments against proportionality that were raised by the Association of Personal Injury Lawyers ("APIL"). Broadly, the concern of APIL was that proportionality of costs to the amount of compensation in personal injury cases would, for two reasons, lead experienced senior personal injury lawyers to give up personal injury work. First, APIL argued that insurers customarily expend large sums in defending small personal injury claims. The work funded by this expenditure on the defendant side could place an intolerable burden on a Plaintiff's lawyer who will know that he can only hope to recover very limited costs. Second, it was argued that the recovery of disproportionate cost is immaterial in the sense that most personal injury actions succeed and successful Plaintiffs will generally recover their costs from the unsuccessful Defendant's insurers. The Report deals with the first point by emphasizing that the envisaged limitation of procedure would automatically limit the work to be done and, therefore, the costs. It emphasized that if an action was unreasonably bankrolled by a Defendant's insurers then a Judge would have the power to disapply the limit on costs. Clearly, this would require Judges to make greater use of their punitive costs discretion than did District Judges under the old small claims jurisdiction (CCR Ord 19, r 4(2)(c)). The Report goes on to reject APIL's second argument on the basis that a system which customarily pays those who advise accident victims more than the victims themselves recover in compensation will justifiably fail to command public confidence. The Report makes it clear that it saw APIL's second line of attack as an assault upon the core of the proposed reforms (Final Report, see Chapter 2, *Fast Track:* General, p 26).

Finally, APIL suggested on consultation that greater access to justice had already been achieved by means of conditional fee agreements which provide Plaintiffs with complete certainty as to costs in that insurance pays the Defendant's costs if the Plaintiff loses and the Plaintiff's solicitor pays his own costs. Conversely, if the Plaintiff wins then he recovers 85% of his costs from the Defendant and pays his own solicitor a success fee. APIL rejected the proposed scheme of fixed recoverable costs on the basis that the cost of litigating could well exceed the level at which the costs were fixed and, in cases of this kind, the Plaintiff would have to top-up the money recovered from the Defendant by either dipping into his own damages or by persuading his solicitor to work for less. The result of this, in APIL's view, was either that Plaintiffs would cease using conditional fee agreements or that experienced personal injury litigators would stop working in the field. The response to this concern in the Report is far from convincing. It states simply that an acceptable costs regime will provide "*a realistic and fair reward*" for litigating cases. While this is, perhaps, an adequate description of the guiding principles of the costs reform it does little, if anything, to articulate any response to the concern raised by APIL in connection with fixed costs and conditional fees.

Chapter 2

The Fast Track Rules: Transitional Arrangements and General Features

The scheme of the Rules: commencement and uniformity

The Civil Procedure Rules 1998 came into force on 26 April 1999. The Pre-action Protocols for personal injury and clinical dispute (medical negligence) claims were published in January 1999 and will be considered for all cases commenced on or after 26 April where it would have been possible for the parties to comply with the tenets of the Protocol during the period between publication and commencement of the Rules. Practitioners were introduced early to a Practice Direction on the costs of short interlocutory hearings and, in the experience of this writer, adapted quickly and efficiently to the preparation of costs schedules and the pre-hearing exchange of the same.

The Rules are divisible into the Rules themselves, numbered in Parts, and the more detailed explanatory Practice Directions that supplement each Rule. In the text that follows the Rules are referred to in brackets by the formula "CPR". Thus, a reference to rule 28.2(2)(a) (*viz.* fixing the trial date in a fast track case) is expressed as "CPR 28.2(2)(a)". Similarly, a reference to the Practice Direction that supplements nearly every separate Part of the Rules is expressed in the text below by use of the formula "Part 28, PD 3.6(1)(b)" (*viz.* agreed directions to fix the trial date).

The Rules contain transitional arrangements for claims commenced before 26 April 1999, which have not, by that date, been dealt with. There will be a long-stop of 12 months for the application of the Rules to all claims; thus, by 26 April 2000, all claims will be "*Woolf claims*". During the 12 month transitional period that precedes this claims commenced before 26 April 1999, will be "*Woolfed*" at an appropriate stage in the proceedings (Part 51, PD 15(1)). This will likely be done at directions hearings (although the number of these interlocutory appointments will be kept to a bare minimum for all fast track claims, for which see below). Where an application is made in a pre-Woolf claim after 26 April 1999, it must be made in accordance with the Rules (Part 51, PD 14(1)).

Those pre-Woolf claims that have not had a trial date fixed and have not been "*Woolfed*" before 25 April 2000, will be automatically stayed (Part 51, PD 19(1)). The general principle of automatic stay does not apply to personal injury claims where there is no issue on liability and where the claim has been adjourned by court order to determine the prognosis.

It should be noted that all costs applications brought before the court after 26 April 1999 should be made and dealt with in accordance with the Rules (Part 51, PD 18). However, the fast track fixed costs regime does not apply until a claim has been formally allocated to the fast track (CPR 44.9(2)).

A number of existing provisions of the County Court Rules (and the Rules of the Supreme Court) are retained in schedules to the new Civil Procedure Rules. Schedule 2 to the Rules contains those of the County Court Rules that are carried forward (at least for the time being) into the new framework. While the bulk of the old County Court Rules have been jettisoned, the provisions on enforcement have essentially been retained. Enforcement is, at the time of writing, still being studied by the Rules Committee and will (probably) be subject to a new scheme of Rules sometime after the dawn of the new millennium.

A key aspect of the "*big bang*" change on 26 April 1999 is that there will be no carrying forward at all of the existing case law. Similarly, local practice directions of the kind promulgated by *ad hoc* committees of the local judiciary will be discouraged as militating against uniformity. The observations of Lord Halsbury LC in *Bank of England* v *Vagliano Brothers* [1891] AC 107 (HL(E)) at p. 120, are, in this context, apposite:

> It seems to me that, construing the statute by adding to it words which are neither found therein nor for which authority could be found in the language of the statute itself, is to sin against one of the most familiar rules of construction, and I am wholly unable to adopt the view that, where a statute is expressly said to codify the law, you are at liberty to go outside the code so created, because before the existence of that code another law prevailed.

One of the few things that can confidently be predicted about the Rules post-26 April is that, within a fairly short period of time, they will become as encumbered with case law annotations as was Order 17, rule 11 of the County Court Rules. Save for this, the form that the Rules will take in practice and the manner in which (as yet) unanticipated problems of construction will be resolved is almost entirely open to question.

The Fast Track: principal characteristics

The Fast Track is about cheap and fast litigation. Litigation stripped of interlocutory proceedings, with a minimal number of court appearances before trial, with standard directions, a strict timetable and fixed costs. The Rules prescribe a series of gates through which it is envisaged each personal injury claim will proceed on the road to trial and beyond:

- the Pre-action Protocol for personal injury claims;
- the commencement of proceedings by claim form and the response to the same;
- the allocation of the claim to the appropriate track;
- the agreement or imposition of directions;
- applications for interim orders;
- trial;
- the recovery of costs.

Clearly, it is of vital importance that a case be allocated early to the most appropriate track. The directions contained in the Rules are tailored specifically for each of the three tracks and delay and costs sanctions will follow if a case is not properly allocated.

Chapter 3

Getting Started: Pre-Action Protocol and Commencing Proceedings

Pre-action protocol for personal injury claims

A principal feature of the Woolf reforms was the desire to encourage the avoidance of litigation and the use of settlement and alternative methods of dispute resolution. It was with this in mind that the drafters of the Rules devised a *"deliberately simple"* and easy to use Pre-action Protocol for personal injury claims which is designed to facilitate contact and the early disclosure of information by the parties with a view to the pre-action settlement of a claim. The principal requirements of the regime are as follows:

- the proposed Claimant shall send the proposed Defendant two copies of a letter in standard form (*"the letter of claim"*);
- the letter will set out a clear summary of the facts on which the claim is based and should also indicate the nature of the injuries suffered and the financial loss sustained;
- the letter should ask for the proposed Defendant's insurance details and request that the Defendant send a copy of the letter to his insurers (it is suggested that a copy of the letter of claim should be provided to the Defendant free of charge for him to send to his insurers);
- the Defendant should provide insurance details (*"acknowledgement of claim"*) within 21 days of the letter of claim and, in default of the same, the Claimant shall be entitled to issue proceedings;
- the Defendant and/or his insurers will have a maximum of three months from the acknowledgement of claim in which to

investigate the claim and should then respond admitting or denying liability (*"letter of reply"*);

- if the Defendant denies liability then he should enclose, with the letter of reply, documents in his possession which are material to the Claimant's claim and which would likely be disclosed post-commencement of proceedings (see, *Pre-action Protocol for Personal Injury Claims*, Annex B which contains standard disclosure lists for fast track cases – these are considered in greater detail below in *Fast Track Directions*, Chapter 5 below which deals with disclosure).

The protocol also makes provision for the joint instruction of experts with a requirement that before a party instructs an expert he must provide the other party with a list of the suitable experts in the relevant speciality. Within 14 days of the service of the list the other party should then raise an objection to any of the experts on the list. The party that compiled the list will then instruct a mutually acceptable expert unless the other party objects to all of the experts on the list in which case the court will instruct an expert. In the event that proceedings are commenced the court is empowered to consider whether either or both parties have acted unreasonably in connection with the instruction of experts (Protocol, para 3.17). In the absence of any objection by the other party to the experts on the list the same party will be obliged to rely on that expert evidence unless: (1) the list compiling party agrees to the instruction of another expert; or (2) the court directs the same; or (3) the list compiling party's expert has amended a report and the original report is not disclosed.

The Rules clearly contemplate the imposition of a costs sanction if, when proceedings are subsequently commenced, it comes to light that a party has failed to comply with a protocol. The Rules state:

> The Courts will be able to treat the standards set in protocols as the normal reasonable approach to pre-action conduct. If proceedings are issued, it will be for the court to decide whether non-compliance with a protocol should merit adverse consequences. Guidance on the court's likely approach will be given from time to time in practice directions.
>
> If the court has to consider the question of compliance after proceedings have begun, it will not be concerned with minor infringements, *eg.* failure by a short period to provide relevant information. One minor breach will not exempt the 'innocent' party from following the protocol. The court

will look at the effect of non-compliance on the other party when deciding whether to impose sanctions.

(Pre-action Protocol for Personal Injury Claims, Introduction, paras 1.4–1.5)

Commencing proceedings

Part 7 of the Rules is headed *"How to Start Proceedings – the Claim Form"*. A claim cannot be commenced in the High Court unless the financial value of the same exceeds £15,000; personal injury claims cannot be commenced in the High Court unless the financial value of the claim exceeds £50,000 (CPR 7.1; Part 7, PD 2.1–2.2). The financial value of the claim is calculated, as under the former system, in accordance with the terms of paragraph 9 of the High Court and County Courts Jurisdiction Order 1991 (SI 1991/724) (see, Part 7, PD 2.2); that is, the sum which the Claimant can reasonably state to be the financial worth of the claim to him.

Statements of case

Pleadings are henceforth collectively renamed *"statements of case"*. Statements of case, amendments of the same and witness statements are to be accompanied by a *"statement of truth"* attesting that the party proffering the statement of case or the party making the witness statement believes the contents of the same to be true. The statement should identify the document (the veracity of which is stated) and should be signed. The statement is usually best included in the document to which it relates. Where a party is legally represented his representative can sign the statement of truth on his behalf, but the statement will attest to the party's, rather than the legal representative's, belief (Part 22, PD 3.7). A statement of case that is not accompanied by a statement of truth will remain effective unless struck out, but cannot be used as evidence (CPR 22.2(1)). The statement of case will also be vulnerable to striking out (CPR 22.2(2)). It is clear that the time-honoured rule that a party should not plead matters of evidence is no more: a statement of case accompanied by a statement of truth *is* evidence. It should be noted that a false statement puts its maker in contempt of Court (CPR 32.14). Practitioners should be particularly wary of signing statements of truth for their clients.

The parties

Part 21 deals with children and patients as parties to litigation. Again, there are changes in nomenclature to be mastered. Guardians *ad litem* and next friends have gone and are collectively replaced by *"litigation friend."* A child remains a person under 18 years of age and a patient is defined by the Rules as

> a person who by reason of mental disorder within the meaning of the Mental Health Act 1983 is incapable of managing and administering his own affairs.

> (CPR 21.1(2))

Insofar as the headings of statements of case are concerned, a child party should be referred to as JOHN SMITH, a Child, by DAVID SMITH, his litigation friend. A patient should be referred to as JOHN SMITH, by DAVID SMITH, his litigation friend. As under the old rules, settlements for children and patients are subject to the approval of the court (CPR 21.10).

Errors in the identification of the parties at commencement can be dealt with under Part 19 of the Rules which makes provision for the addition and substitution of parties. The court can order a person to be added as a new party if:

- this is desirable to enable all the matters in dispute in the proceedings to be resolved; or
- this is desirable to enable the resolution of an issue which is connected to the proceedings and which involves the new party and an existing party

(CPR 19.1(2)).

There is a very similar provision in the Rules for the removal of a party (CPR 19.1(3)) and for the substitution of a new party for an existing one (CPR 19.1(4)). The procedure for the removal, addition or substitution of a party is straightforward and the attention of readers is directed to the relevant section of the Rules (CPR 19.3). Personal injury practitioners should pay particular attention to that section of Part 19 that makes special provision for adding and substituting parties after the end of a relevant limitation period. This provides that an application of this kind after the end of a period of limitation under the Limitation Act 1980 may only be made if the proceedings were commenced at a time when the relevant limitation period was current and if the addition or substitution is necessary (CPR 19.4(2)). The necessity of the addition or substitution of new parties is defined closely by the Rules. Such amendment will be necessary if:

- the new party is to be substituted for a party named by mistake in the claim form;
- the claim cannot properly be carried on by or against an existing party unless the new party is added or substituted as the Claimant or Defendant;
- an existing party has died or been made bankrupt and his interest or liability has passed to the new party. (CPR 19.4(3)).

The Rules make particular provision for personal injury cases. They provide that in a claim of this kind the court can add or substitute a party where it directs that sections 11 (time-limit for personal injury claims) or 12 (time-limit for fatal accidents claims) of the Limitation Act 1980 shall not apply to the claim by or against the new party (CPR 19.4(4)(a)). The question whether those sections should apply will be determined at the trial of the claim (CPR 19.4(4)(b)).

The Claim form and particulars of claim: content and time limits

Proceedings are *"started"* when the court issues a claim form at the Claimant's request and a claim form is issued on the date stamped on its front by the Court (CPR 7.2). The claim form must contain the following:

- a concise statement of the nature of the claim;
- the remedy sought by the Claimant;
- a statement of the estimated financial value of the claim (CPR 16.2(1)).

The claim form must be served on the Defendant within four months of the date of issue (six months if the claim form is to be served outside the jurisdiction) (CPR 7.5). The particulars of the Claimant's claim, which will continue to be called the "*Particulars of Claim*", must either be contained in the claim form itself, or may, alternatively, be served separately on the Defendant within 14 days of the service of the claim form (CPR 7.4(1)). If served separately, the Particulars of Claim must be filed by the Claimant, with certificate of service, within seven days of service on the Defendant (CPR 7.4(3)). The Particulars of Claim, if not contained in the Claim form itself, must not be served on the Defendant any later than the latest permitted time for serving the Claim form on the Defendant (CPR 7.4(2)). The Particulars of Claim, whether set out in the claim form itself, or separately, must also be accompanied by a form for defending the claim, a form for admitting the claim and a form for acknowledging service (CPR 7.8(1)).

It is possible for a Claimant to apply for an extension of time for serving the claim form. As a general rule this must be done by application within the four month period for serving the form, or within the period of any extension already granted (CPR 7.6(2)). In circumstances where the Claimant has failed to apply for an extension within the time permitted for service an order for an extension may only be made if the court has failed to serve the claim form on the Defendant, or if the Claimant has taken all reasonable steps to effect service and yet has failed to do so (CPR 7.6(3)). In either case the Claimant must act promptly (CPR 7.6(3)(c)). An application for an extension may be made without giving notice to the proposed Defendant and must be supported by evidence (CPR 7.6(4)).

In personal injury claims the Particulars of Claim must contain the following:

- the Claimant's date of birth;
- brief details of the Claimant's personal injuries (Part 16, PD 4.1).

In addition, a schedule of details of any past and future expenses and losses claimed should be attached to the Particulars of Claim. Similarly, where reliance is placed on evidence from a medical practitioner, a report by the same should be attached to the Particulars of Claim (Part 16, PD 4.2–4.3). If a claim is made for provisional damages then the Claimant must state in his Particulars of Claim, as under the old Rules:

(1) that he seeks an award under section 32A of the Supreme Court Act 1981 or section 51 of the County Courts Act 1984;
(2) that there is a chance that at some future time he will develop some serious disease or suffer some serious deterioration in his physical or mental condition;
(3) the disease or type of deterioration in respect of which an application may be made at a future date (Part 16, PD 4.4).

If the claim is brought under the Fatal Accidents Act 1976 this must be spelt out in the Particulars of Claim (Part 16, PD 5.1–5.3).

In cases where the claim is based on a written agreement the same must be attached to the Particulars of Claim and the original must be available at the hearing (Part 16, PD 9.3(1)). Where the relevant agreement is alleged to have been concluded orally or by conduct the Claimant must specify the words or conduct relied upon (Part 16, PD 9.4–9.5). If the Claimant wishes to rely upon evidence of a person's conviction of a criminal offence then the Particulars of Claim must contain details of the court that convicted that person, together with the type and date of the conviction (Part 16, PD 10.1). The Claimant must also identify the issue to which the conviction relates.

The Defence: content and time-limits

The Rules provide that, in his Defence, the Defendant must state the following:

- which of the allegations in the Particulars of Claim he denies;
- which of the allegations he is unable to admit or deny, but which he requires the Claimant to prove;
- which of the allegations he admits (CPR 16.5(1)).

The Rules further provide that where an allegation has been denied the Defendant must give his reasons for doing so and must, where he makes averments of a different version of events than the Claimant, set out his own version of events (CPR 16.5(2)). The Rules state that a Defendant who fails expressly to deal with an allegation, but who states his own case in relation to it, is to be taken implicitly to put the Claimant to proof on that allegation (CPR 16.5(3)). Subject to this concession, if a Defendant fails to deal with an allegation in the Particulars of Claim he is taken to have admitted the same (CPR 16.5(5)). If the Defendant disputes the Claimant's statement of the value of his claim then he should try, if he is able, to make his own assessment of the financial value of the Claimant's claim (CPR 16.5(6)). The Rules contain straightforward and uncharacteristically succinct provisions dealing with Defence of set-off and Reply to a Defence (CPR 16.6–16.7). A counterclaim can be made by the Defendant against the Claimant by filing particulars of the same with his Defence (in which case permission of the court is *not* required) or at any other time (in which case permission of the court *is* required) (CPR 20.4(1)–(2)).

The Practice Direction to Part 16 of the Rules contains some detailed provisions for matters to be included in Defences in personal injury claims. It provides that, in cases where the Claimant has attached a medical report in respect of his injuries, the Defendant should state whether he agrees, disputes or is unable to plead to the matters set out in the medical report (Part 16, PD 14.1(1)). If the medical report is disputed then reasons for this should be given in the Defence (Part 16, PD 14.1(2)). Where the Defendant has obtained his own medical report, on which he proposes to rely, then he should attach this to his Defence (Part 16, PD 14.1(3)). It will, of course, be quite unusual for a Defendant to obtain a separate medical report in fast track claims; a single joint expert will be the norm. The Defendant should also include similar particulars in his Defence in respect of the Plaintiff's schedule of past and future expenses and losses where the content of this is disputed (Part 16, PD 14.2).

Generally, a Defence must be filed 14 days after service of the Particulars of Claim or 28 days after service of the Particulars of Claim if the Defendant files an acknowledgement of service (CPR 15.4). The Rules contain provision for the parties to agree to an extension of 28 days for the service of the Defence; in these circumstances, the Defendant must notify the court of the extension in writing (CPR 15.5).

The Rules curtail the number of statements of case (pleadings) that may be filed and served without leave by providing expressly that no further statement of case may be served after the Reply without the permission of the court (CPR 15.9).

Third party claims

Part 20 of the Rules deals with third party proceedings which were to be re-named. At the time of writing it appears that an original suggestion that they be called *"Part 20 claims"* has now been adopted. The prefatory remarks to Part 20 read, *"A Part 20 claim is any claim other than the claim by the claimant against the defendant."* The allocation rules set out below do not expressly apply to Part 20 claims, but the procedural judge is directed to ensure, so far as the same is possible, that the Part 20 claim is managed together with the claim (CPR 20.13(2)).

Further information

Requests for Further and Better Particulars and Interrogatories are no more: both are now collectively known as *"Further Information"* and are dealt with in Part 18 of the Rules. The Court is empowered to order any party to clarify any matter in dispute or to give additional information in relation to any matter (CPR 18.1). The relevant Practice Direction prescribes the procedure for applications for the same (Part 18, PD).

Chapter 4

Allocation to the Fast Track

General features

Part 26 of the Rules, snappily headed *"Case Management – Preliminary Stage"*, contains provisions for the allocation of defended claims to the most appropriate track. The general landscape is as follows:

- once a Defence is filed both parties must complete an allocation questionnaire – Form N150 (CPR 26.3(1));
- the parties must complete an allocation questionnaire within the time-limit provided by the court which must be at least 14 days after the deemed date of service (CPR 26.3(6));
- at the same time that an allocation questionnaire is completed a party can make a written request that the proceedings be stayed for one month or longer in order to provide an opportunity for alternative dispute resolution (CPR 26.4(1));
- the court may – with or without an allocation hearing – allocate the case to a track once the parties have filed questionnaires, or once the time for filing questionnaires has passed (CPR 26.5));
- there is a presumption that the fast track will be the correct track for personal injury claims where the financial value of damages for pain, suffering and loss of amenity exceeds £1,000, but the financial value of the total claim for damages does not exceed £15,000 (CPR 26.6(4)) *and where*:
- the trial is likely to last no longer than one day; and
- oral expert evidence will be limited to one expert per party in relation to any expert field and expert evidence in two expert fields (CPR 26.6(5)).

The questionnaire

The court is empowered to dispense with the requirement to serve a questionnaire (CPR 26.3(1)). For example, if an early summary judgment application is made the court may, on dismissal of the application, hold an allocation hearing and dispense with the need for completion of a questionnaire. In addition to a general discretion to dispense with this requirement the court will not serve a questionnaire if the claim is for a specified sum of money and the Defendant states that he has already paid the claimed sum (CPR 15.10) or if the claim is for a specified sum of money and the Defendant admits part of the claim (CPR 14.5). If there is more than one Defendant then the court will serve questionnaires once all the Defendants have filed their Defences (CPR 26.3(2)).

A practice direction supplementing rule 26 provides that the court will not consider information provided by a party as a matter alleged to affect allocation unless the document containing the information certifies that the parties agree that the information provided is correct and should be put before the court or if it confirms that the party tendering the information has delivered a copy to the other parties (PD 2.2(2)). The practice direction goes on to state that parties should consult and co-operate over the completion of the allocation questionnaire, provided that such consultation does not delay the submission of the questionnaire to the court (PD 2.3). The parties should also attempt to agree the directions that they will invite the court to make on allocation (PD 2.3(2)).

If no allocation questionnaire is received from either party within the time-limit then the court is empowered to give any direction it thinks appropriate (CPR 26.5(5)). The practice direction makes it clear that this will usually include an impromptu "unless" order that the claim and any counterclaim be struck out if no questionnaire is submitted within three days (PD 2.5(1)). If only one party submits an allocation questionnaire within time the court can allocate the case if it has sufficient information to do so and, if not, can order attendance by both parties at an allocation hearing (PD 2.5(2)). The party in default will usually be ordered to pay indemnity costs of the hearing which will be summarily assessed by the court (PD 6.6(2)(a)). A time-limit can be set for the payment of those costs with a sanction for defaulters that the claim or counterclaim be struck out (PD 6.6(2)(b)).

If the allocation hearing is held on the court's initiative then the court should give seven days' notice to the parties (Form N153) (PD 6.2). The notice requirement will not apply if the court treats another interlocutory hearing as an allocation hearing (PD 6.3).

Stay of proceedings for alternative dispute resolution

A party can – by letter of request – ask for a stay of proceedings at the same time as filing the allocation questionnaire and the court is empowered of its own motion to stay proceedings (CPR 26.4(2)). The letter should generally state that the request for a stay is made with the agreement of all the parties and should also explain the steps being taken to achieve the settlement of the case. The object of the stay is the same in both cases: to enable the parties to settle the case by alternative dispute resolution or other means (CPR 26.4(1)). This is succinctly defined by the glossary to the Rules as the, *"collective description of methods of resolving disputes otherwise than through the normal trial process."*

The general period of the stay is one month which can be extended for such period as the court thinks appropriate (CPR 26.4(3)). At the end of the period of stay the court will give directions for the management of the case (CPR 26.4(5)) which may include the allocation of the case to a track or the ordering of an allocation hearing.

The appropriate track

The principal determinant of track-allocation is the financial value of the claim. Financial value is calculated by disregarding: (1) any amounts claimed which are not in dispute; (2) interest; (3) costs; (4) contributory negligence (CPR 26.8(2)). The court is charged with the responsibility of assessing the financial value of the claim. Any claim worth less than £15,000 will normally be dealt with by the fast track, rather than by the multi track (CPR 26.6(4)(b)). Any action with a claim for pain, suffering and loss of amenity which is estimated to exceed £1,000 will normally be dealt with under the fast track, rather than the small claims track (CPR 26.6(1)(a)(ii)). While the financial value of the claim will be employed to set the *"normal"* track for the management of the case, the court will look to a range of other factors to determine whether or not a case should be allocated to the normal track (CPR 26.7). Cases that are estimated to last longer than a day (defined as five hours of court time) are not generally suitable for the fast track (CPR 26.6(5)(a)). Cases requiring a number of expert witnesses are not generally suitable for the fast track (CPR 26.6(5)(b)), nor are cases in which a party might be materially disadvantaged by the limitations on disclosure imposed in fast track cases. The following relevant factors are set out in the Rules (CPR 26.8(1)):

- financial value;
- the remedy sought;
- the complexity of the facts, law or evidence;
- the number of parties, or likely parties;
- the value of any counterclaim and the complexity of the issues surrounding it;
- the amount of oral evidence;
- the public importance of the case;
- the parties' views;
- the parties' circumstances.

The relevant factors are listed hierarchically. It is, of course, of more than merely symbolic importance that the financial value of the claim is listed first and the parties' own views second to last. In spite of this the information contained on the allocation questionnaire, the manner in which the information is presented and the views of the parties must have a significant impact upon the decision made by the court. The allocation questionnaire asks parties to indicate the most suitable track and then, *"If you have indicated a track which would not be the normal track for your case, please give brief reasons for your choice."*

The Rules empower the court to request more information from a party if the information set out in the questionnaire does not provide it with sufficient material on which to base an allocation decision (CPR 26.5(3)). The practice direction also suggests that the court should use this power to order a party to provide more information in circumstances where it is sceptical about the estimate of the financial value of a claim given by a party (Part 26, PD 4.2(2)). The days of speculative estimates of value tagged onto the end of a Particulars of Claim would appear to be numbered. The practice direction makes it clear that the parties cannot oust the court's jurisdiction to allocate on the basis of any common agreement between them as to the most appropriate track, although this will, as indicated above, be *"an important factor"* (Part 26, PD 7.5).

Chapter 5

Fast Track Directions

General features

It is in the context of the directions provisions for fast track cases that the novelty of the new Rules is, perhaps, most apparent. Part 28 of the Rules, headed *"The Fast Track"*, makes provision for fast track directions by setting out a rather skeletal framework within which a case is to be organized. The giving of directions will follow the allocation of a case to the fast track and will provide for the completion of all the steps up to and including the fixing of the trial date or the three week period during which the trial will take place (CPR 28.2(1)–(2)) (*cf.* automatic striking out under the old Rules and the effect of *Ferreira* v *American Embassy Employees' Federation* [1996] 1 WLR 536 (CA), before it was overtaken by *Bannister* v *SGB Plc* [1998] 1 WLR 1123 (CA)). It is clear from both the Rules (CPR 28.5) and the extensive practice direction which supplements them that directions may also be necessary after the parties have filed listing questionnaires. The Rules provide for a standard period between the giving of the directions following allocation and the trial itself: not more than 30 weeks (CPR 28.2(4)). The directions given will include provisions to deal with

(1) disclosure of documents;
(2) service of witness statements;
(3) expert evidence (CPR 28.3(1)).

The practice direction supplementing the Rules provides that the court will generally give directions upon allocation and filing of listing questionnaires without the need for a hearing (Part 28, PD 2.1–2.2); the court may, however, give directions at any interim hearing either on its own initiative or on that of a party (Part 28, PD 2.3–2.4).

Allocation directions

The practice direction indicates that where the parties have agreed case management directions which make clear *and timetabled* provision for the minimal directions requirements contained in the Rules (at CPR 28.2–28.3) the court will ordinarily approve the same (Part 28, PD 3.5).

Disclosure

Disclosure can either be of *"standard"* kind or the parties or court can provide their own bespoke disclosure direction. It is clear that an order for disclosure, without more, will be taken as an order for standard disclosure (CPR 31.5(1)). Standard disclosure is defined to require a party to disclose, after a reasonable search (CPR 31.6):

- the documents on which he relies; and
- the documents which
  - adversely affect his case;
  - adversely affect another party's case; or
  - support another party's case; and
- the documents that he is required to disclose by a relevant practice direction.

The practice direction goes on to provide that it is possible for a direction to be given that disclosure will take place by the supply of copies of the documents without the need for a list to be served, although, in such circumstances, the party serving copies of the documents must serve a disclosure statement (Part 28, PD 3.6(4)(b)). It should, however, be noted that service of a disclosure statement is, in any event, general required practice where standard disclosure is made (see, CPR 31.10(5)). In a case where copies of documents are served in lieu of a formal list, the disclosure statement must:

- expressly state that the party disclosing the documents believes the extent of the search to have been reasonable in all the circumstances;
- set out the extent of the search and, where the same has been limited for reasons of proportionality (*eg.* because the costs of searching out the documents outweighs their importance or

relevance to the matters in dispute), give reasons for the adoption of the limitations;

- if the party making the disclosure statement is a company, firm, association or other organization, the statement must identify the name and address of the person making the statement and explain why he is a suitable person to make the statement (CPR 31.10(7)).

Inspection

Once a document has been disclosed the party to whom it has been disclosed has a right to inspect the same unless the document is no longer in the control of the disclosing party (defined by CPR 31.8) or the disclosing party has a right to withhold the document on public interest grounds (CPR 31.3(1) and 31.19). The principle of proportionality, central to the Rules, also applies to the issue of inspection. If a disclosing party takes the view that it would be disproportionate for him to permit inspection of a document that he has disclosed then he must state the same in his disclosure statement (CPR 31.3(2)).

It is, of course, possible under the Rules for a party to make application for the following orders:

- specific disclosure or inspection (CPR 31.12 and Part 31, PD 5.1–5.4);
- inspection of a document mentioned in a statement of case, witness statement, affidavit etc. (CPR 31.14);
- pre-action disclosure (CPR 31.16);
- non-party disclosure (CPR 31.17).

Further directions

The Practice Direction to Part 28 directs that in fast track claims the parties should also agree directions to deal with the filing of replies or amended statements of case, if any, the dates for service of requests for further information and questions to experts and the use of a single joint expert (Part 28, PD 3.7). If the Court decides that it will give directions itself, or is not aware of any agreed directions, it will generally order the directions set out below which are clearly intended as a template for the most appropriate directions in a fast track claim and should also be regarded as an indication of the sort of agreed directions that the Court will approve (Part 28, PD 3.9). It should be particularly noted that the Court will ordinarily fix the trial date or appropriate trial period (CPR 28.6(1)). The parties will ordinarily be given three weeks notice of the date fixed (CPR 28.6(2)). The general directions that a Court will make are as follows:

- directions for filing or service of any further information required to clarify a party's case;
- standard disclosure;
- simultaneous exchange of witness statements;
- a joint single expert;
- in the absence of a joint single expert, simultaneous exchange of expert's reports;
- fixing a trial date or trial period.

The Practice Direction contains a suggested timetable for the path that a claim will take to trial (Part 28, PD 3.12). This gives a clear indication as to the abbreviated nature of fast track proceedings (all of the periods set out below run from the date of the notice of allocation):

ACTION	PERIOD FROM DATE OF NOTICE OF ALLOCATION
Disclosure	4 weeks
Exchange of witness statements	10 weeks
Exchange of expert's reports (if more than one)	14 weeks
Sending of listing questionnaire by court	20 weeks
Filing of completed listing questionnaire	22 weeks
Hearing	30 weeks

The Court is specifically empowered to omit any of the steps set out above, if the same is considered to be unnecessary, with a view to ensuring that the case arrives even more speedily at the trial hearing (Part 28, PD 3.13(1)).

Varying the directions order

Any party aggrieved by a direction should, as soon as possible and within 14 days of the service of the Order, either appeal against the Order (if he was present at the hearing when the Order was made) or apply for reconsideration of the same (if the Order was made in his absence) (Part 28, PD 4.1–4.4). There is provision in the Practice Direction for the parties to agree a change to the Order for directions (see, Part 28, PD 4.5).

Failure to comply with directions

The Practice Direction provides that where there has been default the *"innocent"* party can apply to the Court (and should do so without delay, giving warning to the defaulting party) for an Order to enforce compliance and/or for a (costs) sanction (Part 28, PD 5.1–5.4). Practitioners should note the effect of that provision of the Rules dealing with relief from costs sanctions which states, *inter alia*, that when considering whether to grant relief from a sanction the Court will examine whether the defaulting party is a recidivist defaulter when it comes to Pre-action Protocols, directions Orders and/or Practice Directions (CPR 3.9(1)(e)).

The principles relevant to the exercise of the Court's powers in respect of applications for postponements will be relatively familiar to those practitioners who experienced the application of *The Mortgage Corporation* v *Sandoes* [1997] PNLR 263 (CA) under the old Rules. Again, the Rules provide that the preservation of the trial date or, where appropriate, the trial period is sacrosanct (Part 28, PD 5.4(1)–(2)). The Court is empowered to order that the trial of those issues that are ready for trial should, where possible, take place on the date fixed for trial leaving any other issues to be tried separately (Part 28, PD 5.4(4)). If the Court has no option but to postpone the trial it must do so for the shortest time possible with directions for any outstanding steps to be taken as rapidly as possible (Part 28, PD 5.4(5)). This part of the Practice Direction concludes with the following stern injunction (Part 28, PD 5.4(6)):

> Litigants and lawyers must be in no doubt that the court will regard the postponement of a trial as an order of last resort. The court may exercise its power to require a party as well as his legal representative to attend court at a hearing where such an order is to be sought.

Chapter 6

Applications, Summary Disposal and Summary Judgment

Applications and interim remedies

Part 23 of the Rules deals with the general formalities for the making of an application to Court both before and after proceedings have commenced. Part 24 contains provisions for summary judgment and Part 25 lists, non-exhaustively, the range of interim remedies that are available to the Court on the making of an application. These matters are dealt with in short form in this book not only because these Parts of the Rules make especially dull reading, but also because the expedited time-table for fast track cases, and the general bias in the Rules against pre-trial hearings, mean that there will be very few opportunities for parties to indulge in interlocutory skirmishing before trial.

Part 23 formalities

The matters of form and content in Part 23 do not make light reading and the reader wishing for detailed guidance as to these matters is best directed to the Rules themselves and the Practice Direction that supplements Part 23. The following general points will suffice:

- applications should be made as soon as the need for the same becomes apparent (Part 23, PD 2.7);
- an application is made by filing and serving an application notice (CPR 23.3(1));
- the application notice will set out the order sought and the reasons for seeking it (CPR 23.6);
- the application notice will generally be accompanied by written evidence that will be served on the respondent and filed with the Court (CPR 23.7(2)–(3));

- if an application is accompanied by a statement of truth it can in itself stand as evidence (CPR Part 22, 23.6 and Part 23, PD 9.7);
- the application notice and any evidence in support should generally be served as soon as possible after filing and not less than three days before the hearing (CPR 23.7(1)(b));
- applications may be heard by telephone conference as well as by "*live*" hearing (Part 23, PD 6.1–6.3);
- wherever possible applications should be made so that they can be considered at some other hearing (for example, at an allocation or listing hearing) (Part 23, PD 2.8);
- applications may be made without serving an application notice in cases of extreme urgency, where the overriding objective is best furthered by the same and with the consent of the court (Part 23, PD 3).

The range of interim remedies

Another change of name: *interlocutory* remedies become "*interim*" remedies under the Rules. Part 25 sets out only a number of the interim remedies that may be sought and these are summarized below. A number of other Parts deal with the other remedies (those not gathered in Part 25) that a party may seek before trial and attention is directed to the following (location guide) table.

INTERIM REMEDY	CPR PART
Order to add or substitute a party	Part 19
Order to amend a statement of case	Part 17
Order for summary judgment	Part 24
Order for further information (formerly Requests for Further and Better Particulars and Interrogatories)	Part 18

Part 25 of the Rules commences with a non-exhaustive list of the most common kinds of interim remedies which will be available under the

Rules. Included among these are orders for:

- inspection of property;
- the taking of a sample of property;
- a freezing injunction (formerly, a *Mareva*);
- a search order (formerly, an *Anton Piller*);
- pre-action disclosure or inspection under section 52 of the County Courts Act 1984;
- non-party disclosure or inspection under section 53 of the County Courts Act 1984;
- an interim payment.

Among the most common situations in which interim remedies will be sought in personal injury cases will be difficulties arising from non-compliance with the Pre-action Protocol. In this situation the best advice that can be given to the *"innocent"* party, aggrieved by the other side's default, is to issue an application for directions. This can be done before commencement or can be dealt with after commencement at a case management conference.

Interim payments

The Rules contain complicated provisions for interim payments which differ little from the position under the old Rules. The formalities require that an application for an interim payment cannot be made before the end of the period for filing an acknowledgement of service (CPR 25.6(1)). The application notice must be served at least 14 days before the hearing of the application and must be supported by evidence (CPR 25.6(3)). Any evidence in response from the Respondent must be filed and served not less than seven days before the hearing of the application (CPR 25.6(4)). The Rules make further provision for evidence in reply to be filed and served at least three days before the application is heard (CPR 26.6(5)).

The test to be satisfied before the Court will make an interim payment is set out in Part 25 (CPR 25.7(1)) and there are few significant differences from the test under the old Rules: the Court must be satisfied, *inter alia*, that, if the claim went to trial, the claimant would obtain judgment for a substantial sum of money (other than costs) against the defendant.

(CPR 25.7(1)(c)).

Additionally, in personal injury cases, the Court may only make an interim payment if:

- the Defendant is insured in respect of the claim; or
- the Defendant's liability will be met by an insurer under the Road Traffic Act 1988; or
- the Defendant is a public body. (CPR 25.7(2)).

As under the old Rules, the Court must not order an interim payment of more than a reasonable proportion of the likely amount of the final judgment and will take into account contributory negligence and any relevant set-off or counterclaim (CPR 25.7(4)–(5)). A separate Practice Direction, supplementing Part 25, deals specifically with interim payments and, *inter alia*, with the compensation recovery unit's potential interest in the same.

Summary disposal

The Court is empowered to strike out a statement of case if:

- it discloses no reasonable grounds for bringing or defending the claim;
- it is an abuse of the Court's process, or is otherwise likely to obstruct the just disposal of the proceedings; or
- there has been a failure to comply with a Rule, a Practice Direction or Court Order. (CPR 3.4(2)).

The last of these three grounds indicates that the making of "*unless*" orders, and striking out for failure to comply with them, may become far more prevalent than under the old Rules (cf. *Hytec Information Systems Limited* v *Coventry City Council* (1996), *The Times*, 31 December). The Practice Direction gives some examples of Particulars of Claim that disclose no reasonable ground for bringing or defending the claim. Among these are, "Money owed £5,000". Also included are Particulars that are incoherent or make no sense and those which contain a coherent set of facts which still do not give rise to a reasonable cause of action

(Part 3, PD 1.4). Defences liable to be struck out will be those that consist of a bare denial, or which do not raise any legally recognized defence (Part 3, PD 1.6). Abusive statements of case will be those which are *"vexatious, scurrilous or obviously ill-founded."* (Part 3, PD 1.5). Court officers are empowered to refer a statement of case to a District Judge at any time if it is considered that the same ought to be disposed of summarily (Part 3, PD 2.1).

Summary judgment

The essential features of applications for summary judgment under the Rules are as follows:

- the summary determination of cases without any realistic prospect of success will be available to the *Defendant*, as well as to the Claimant;
- the test for summary judgment will be the same whether application is made by the Claimant or by the Defendant;
- the Court can take the initiative in raising the question of summary judgment (under CPR 3.3);
- there is no requirement for the application to be supported by evidence in specific form;
- if the application is made by the Claimant, the Defendant is under no burden to show that he has a defence;
- the *"leave to defend"* concept is no more (although the Court can make a conditional order – defined below).

The new provisions of Part 24 are intended to apply to any situation in which the Court determines that a claim or issue can be decided upon without the need for trial (CPR 24.1). Thus, the summary judgment procedure under Part 24 is available to applications based on matters of fact or law. Unless and until a Defendant has filed an acknowledgement of service or a Defence, the application cannot be made without the permission of the Court or the sanction of a Practice Direction (CPR 24.4(1)). The Rules provide that the Court can give summary judgment against a Claimant or Defendant on the whole of the claim, or on a particular issue, if it considers that:

- the Claimant has no realistic prospect of succeeding on the claim or issue; or

- the Defendant has no real prospect of successfully defending the claim or issue; and
- there is no other reason why the case or issue should proceed to trial (for example, a public interest in trial). (CPR 24.2)

The orders available to the Court on an application for summary judgment are set out in the relevant Practice Direction and consist of: judgment on the claim; the striking out or dismissal of the claim; the dismissal of the application; a conditional order (Part 24, PD 5.1). A conditional order is an order requiring a party to pay a sum of money into court or to take any other specified step (Part 24, PD 5.2). If this condition is not complied with the party's claim or statement of case will be dismissed or struck out. If the case is not summarily determined as a result of a Part 24 application the Court will use the hearing as an opportunity to give case management directions (Part 24, PD 10). As elsewhere in the Rules, the emphasis is firmly upon the avoidance of wasted time whenever both parties are, for whatever reason, conveniently present at Court. Practitioners must be prepared for Judges to turn almost any hearing into a directions hearing.

Chapter 7

Evidence: Lay Witnesses and Experts

Lay witnesses: general features

The emphasis in Part 32, which deals with lay witness evidence, is upon the essentials and upon limiting in advance the matters on which witnesses are to give evidence in the interests of saving time and money. These objects are to be achieved by giving the Court power to direct the *issues* on which it requires evidence, the *nature* of the evidence which it requires in order to decide those issues and the *manner* in which the evidence is to be placed before the Court (CPR 32.1(1)). The Court is empowered to use this part of the Rules to exclude evidence that would otherwise be admissible and to limit cross-examination (CPR 32.1(2)–(3)). The Rules state that the general rule is, as before, that witnesses will give oral evidence at trial and written evidence at any other hearing (CPR 32.2). Where a party has served a witness statement and wishes to rely on the evidence of the maker of the statement then he must call the witness at trial or put the statement in as hearsay evidence (for which see, CPR Part 33) (CPR 32.5(1)). The Trial Chapter below deals with the manner in which a witness statement is to be used at trial. In any hearing other than a trial a party will generally use a *witness statement*, rather than an Affidavit, as evidential support for the application (CPR 32.6(1)), but a party can now use his statement of case or application notice as evidence in support of his application, provided that it is accompanied by a Part 22 statement of truth (CPR 32.6(2)).

In cases where a party is required to serve a witness statement by a certain date for use at trial, and is unable to obtain a statement, he may apply for permission to serve a witness summary instead, which will set out in brief the evidence to be given and will contain the name and address of the witness (CPR 32.9). The consequences of a party's failure to serve a witness statement or summary in time are built into the Rules which provide:

If a witness statement or a witness summary for use at trial is not served in respect of an intended witness within the time specified by the court, then the witness may not be called to give oral evidence unless the court gives permission.

(CPR 32.10)

If past form is anything to go by it seems likely that there will be case law to indicate the basis on which the Court might be prepared to give permission (will *The Mortgage Corporation* v *Sandoes* [1997] PNLR 263 CA continue to provide any guidance? – see, Part 28, PD 5.1–5.4).

The form of the witness statement

The Practice Direction supplementing Part 32 sets out the matters of form that must be observed in respect of witness statements. These will henceforth look rather like Affidavits in that they must:

- be headed with the name and number of the proceedings and the Court in which they are proceeding (Part 32, PD 17.1);
- contain, in the top right hand corner of the first page, written details of the party on whose behalf the statement is made, the initials and surname of the witness, the number of the statement in relation to the witness, the initials and number of each exhibit referred to and the date of the statement (Part 32, PD 17.2);
- state the full name, address and occupation of the witness (Part 32, PD 18.1);
- identify the parts of the statement that are made from the witness's information or belief, rather than knowledge (the source of the information or belief should be given) (Part 32, PD 18.2);
- be produced on durable A4 paper with a 3.5 centimetre margin, be typed on one side of the paper, be paginated consecutively and express all numbers in figures (Part 32, PD 19.1);
- include a Part 22 statement of truth (Part 32, PD 20.1–20.3).

The fact that witness statements will now look like Affidavits is a consequence of the rule that they will now generally be used as evidence in support of interim applications. Curiously, given that statements of case can now stand as evidence, if accompanied by a statement of truth, and should, therefore, contain more discursive narrative than before, it may be that witness statements will, correspondingly, be abbreviated and more succinct.

Experts: general features

The main thrust of the Rules, as they touch on expert evidence, is to discourage (and even prohibit) the parties from bringing their own *"pet"* experts to trial. Most fast track personal injury trials will take place with a single, mutually acceptable or Court-appointed, expert witness if they take place with an expert at all. The Chapter above that describes the Pre-action Protocol for personal injury cases will have made it clear that the appointment of the single expert will generally have taken place before proceedings are commenced. It should be noted that the Court will not direct an expert to attend a fast track hearing unless it is necessary in the interests of justice for him to do so (CPR 35.5(2)). Another feature of the fast track system that will, inevitably, impact on the attendance of experts at trial is the strict time table that will apply. If the parties' favourite expert cannot attend on the trial date the Court will expect them to select another expert.

The attenuated nature of expert evidence is emphasized by Part 35 of the Rules which starts by stating that, *"Expert evidence shall be restricted to that which is reasonably required to resolve the proceedings."* (CPR 35.1). The Rules' determination to ensure that this is achieved is made emphatically clear by the fact that an expert can only give evidence with the permission of the Court and that an application for permission to call expert evidence must identify the expert's area of expertise and must, if practicable, give the expert's name (CPR 35.4(1)–(2)). Experts, the Rules state, have an *overriding* duty to help the Court (CPR 35.3). The corollary of this is that experts are now given a right of *direct access* to the Court to obtain directions to assist them with their work (CPR 35.14(1)). It is not necessary for the expert to give notice to the parties before making this application, although the Court can direct that this notice should be given (CPR 35.14(2)–(3)).

The single joint expert

The Court is empowered by the Rules to direct that only one expert should give evidence (CPR 35.7(1)) and where the parties cannot agree who that single expert should be the Court may choose one for them from a list prepared by the parties (CPR 35.7(3)). The Rules provide that a party may put written questions to an expert about his report, provided that the question is put only once and that this is done within 28 days of the service of the report (CPR 35.6). Where written questions are put to an expert, the questioning party should send a copy of the questions to the other party's solicitors at the same time that these are sent to the expert (Part 35, PD 4.2). Pre-trial questioning in writing is likely to be a particularly useful tool in single expert fast track personal injury claims where, as indicated above, the single expert will be the general norm. In these cases both parties can give instructions to the single expert and must send a copy of the instructions to the other party (CPR 35.8(1)–(2)). However, cross-examination of an expert on the contents of his instructions will not be allowed unless the Court grants permission for the same (Part 35, PD 3). The parties instructing the single expert are, unless the Court directs otherwise, jointly and severally liable for his fees (CPR 35.8(5)).

The form of the expert report

The Rules state that expert evidence is to be given in a written report unless the Court directs otherwise (CPR 35.5(1)). In addition the Practice Direction to Part 35 provides that the report must:

- give details of the expert's qualifications;
- gives details of the literature and any other material that the expert has relied on;
- where there is a range of opinion on the matters dealt with in the report, summarize the range and give reasons for the expert's opinion;
- contain a summary of the conclusions;
- contain a statement that the expert understands and has complied with his overriding duty to the Court;
- contain a statement setting out the substance of all material written and oral instructions;

- include a Part 22 statement of truth. (Part 35, PD 1.2–1.3).

Assessors

The Rules also empower the Court to appoint its own assessor to assist it in dealing with any matter in respect of which the assessor has skill and experience (CPR 35.15). Where this is proposed the Court will give the parties full details of the proposed assessor not less than 21 days before the appointment and the parties will have an opportunity to object to the same (Part 35, PD 6.1). If an assessor is appointed and produces a report before the start of the trial the Court will send a copy of the same to the parties (CPR 35.15(4)). The assessor will not, however, give oral evidence at trial and will not be subject to cross-examination on his report (Part 35, PD 6.4). The Court can look to the parties to pay the costs of the assessor (CPR 35.15(5)–(6)). It is very unlikely that assessors will be used at any fast track personal injury trial.

Chapter 8

Offers to Settle and Payments into Court

General features

The new system for offers to settle and payments into court is set out in Part 36 of the Rules. The key innovations are as follows:

- the system has been extended to cover offers in monetary and non-monetary claims;
- the system provides for the payment of interest on the judgment debt and costs (on the indemnity basis) if the Claimant beats the offer to settle or payment in;
- the Claimant is now able to make an offer to settle (that is, to offer to settle his claim for £x) which will be binding on him and can have costs implications.

This Chapter will consider only the procedural formalities and conditions for the making of an offer to settle or a payment into court together with the acceptance of the same. The costs implications of action taken under Part 36 are considered in detail in Chapter 10 below on costs. The Rules refer to the party making the offer (whether Claimant or Defendant) as the *"offeror"* and the party to whom the offer is addressed as the *"offeree"*.

Form and content

The Rules prescribe the formalities for the making of a Part 36 offer or payment and also the consequences of such an offer or payment. Unless the party observes the formalities the court will have to be asked to *order* that the Part 36 consequences should follow (CPR 36.1(2)). It should be noted that the Court can still take account of an offer not made in observance of Part 36 form in deciding whether and how to exercise its discretion as to costs (CPR 44.3(4)(c)).

A Part 36 offer to settle must be in writing, must state whether it relates to the whole claim or part of it, must state whether it takes account of any counterclaim and must state whether it takes account of interest (if it does not state that interest is excluded it will be taken to include interest (CPR 36.5(1)–(3) and Part 36, PD 5.4)). The same formalities as to the provision of information must be observed when a Part 36 notice of a payment in is filed with the Court (CPR 36.6(1)–(2)). The Part 36 offer or payment must state that it is made under Part 36 and must be signed by the offeror party or by his legal representative (Part 36, PD 5.1)). The Court will serve the notice of payment-in on the offeree unless the offeror has served the same, in which case a certificate of service must be provided to the Court. (CPR 36.6(3)–(4)).

It is possible under the Rules for a Defendant to make a payment in respect of a claim for provisional damages (CPR 36.7). If this is done the Defendant must state in his payment notice whether he agrees to the making of an award of provisional damages (CPR 36.7(2)). The payment notice must also state that the sum paid in is in satisfaction of the claim for damages on the assumption that the Claimant will not develop the disease or suffer the type of deterioration specified in the notice. Further, it must state that the offer is subject to the condition that the Claimant makes any claim for further damages within a specified period (it must state what that period is) (CPR 36.7(3)).

The offeree can, within seven days of the Part 36 offer or payment being made, ask for clarification of the same (CPR 36.9(1)) and, if the offeror refuses to clarify, can compel him to do so on application to the Court (CPR 36.9(2)).

The Practice Direction makes provision for compensation recovery and the obtaining by the Defendant of a certificate of recoverable benefits and a Compensation Recovery Unit certificate to be filed with the payment notice (Part 36, PD 10.1–10.5).

Usefully, it is open to a party to make an offer to settle *before* proceedings are commenced (CPR 36.10(1)). The offer will be taken into account by the court when assessing costs. Such pre-action offers to settle must be expressed to be open for at least 21 days after the offer is made and, if made by the prospective Defendant, must include an offer to pay the prospective Claimant's costs for the 21 days after the offer is made (CPR 36.10(2)). Otherwise, the pre-action offer must comply with Part 36 formalities (CPR 36.10(2)(c)).

Time limits

The general rule is that Part 36 offers and payments and the acceptance of the same must take place *not less than 21 days before trial*. It is possible to extend the time for making the offer or payment and acceptance of the same if agreement is reached as to costs liability or if the Court gives its permission for the same. The following table sets out the location of the relevant time limit rules:

OFFER TO SETTLE/PAYMENT INTO COURT	CPR TIME LIMIT RULE
Part 36 Offer to Settle or Payment	CPR 36.5(6)
Acceptance of Defendant's Offer or Payment	CPR 36.11(1)
Acceptance of Claimant's Offer	CPR 36.12(1)

A Part 36 offer is made when it is received by the offeree (CPR 36.8(1)) and a payment is made when the written notice is served on the offeree (CPR 36.8(2)). The same are accepted when notice of acceptance is received by the offeror (CPR 36.8(5)). The notice of acceptance must set out the claim number, the title of the proceedings, must identify the Part 36 offer or payment notice and must be signed by the offeree or by his legal representative (Part 36, PD 7.7). It should be noted that where a party is legally represented the Part 36 offer, payment notice and notice of acceptance must be served on the party's legal representative as well as on the party (Part 36, PD 11.1).

A part 36 offer or payment made less than 21 days before the start of trial cannot be accepted without the court's permission unless the parties have agreed terms as to costs (Part 36, PD 7.3). Permission is sought by Part 23 application or at trial (Part 36, PD 7.4). Where a payment is accepted with permission the parties will require an Order for payment-out (Part 36, PD 7.8). Interest on sums paid out is to be dealt with as under the old rules.

Consequences of a Part 36 offer or payment

Action taken by a party pursuant to Part 36 is taken without prejudice save as to costs and will, of course, be kept from the trial judge until liability and quantum have been determined (CPR 36.19(1)–(2)). If a Part 36 offer or payment relates to the whole claim and is accepted then the claim is stayed (CPR 36.15(1)). If the offer or payment relates only to part of the claim that part of the claim *only* will be stayed (CPR 36.15(3)(a)) and the Court will decide the liability as to costs unless the parties have reached agreement as to the same (CPR 36.15(3)(b)).

The chief consequence of the making and acceptance of a Part 36 offer to settle or payment will be in respect of costs and, as indicated above, this is dealt with in Chapter 10 below on costs.

Chapter 9

The Fast Track Trial

General features

The defining characteristic of the fast track trial is that it will be *fast*. The time between commencement and trial will, as we have already seen, be short. The length of the trial will also, necessarily, be short. In order for this to be possible it will be vitally important that each case is carefully prepared ahead of time. Trial bundles must contain only the important documents and be properly paginated. Witness statements should contain all of the relevant evidence-in-chief; there will not be time at trial for anything other than brief supplementary examination. Costs bundles and a schedule of costs claimed should be available at Court and the costs schedule must be exchanged with the other side in advance of the hearing. Perhaps, most interestingly, the truncated nature of the fast track trial and the fact that the costs of over-running cannot be recovered from the party paying costs, means that a new style of advocacy will be necessary. Advocates will have to curb any tendency towards verbosity and they will have to concentrate even more on the careful preparation of cross-examination (already a key feature of the civil trial) with a view to making the best use of the very limited time available to them. A cultural change is also required from the judiciary. The more interventionist Judge may well find his questioning of a witness being challenged by an advocate whose own time with that witness is being used up. The key features of the new regime as it applies to trial are as follows:

- the listing questionnaire;
- postponing the trial (only exceptionally possible, as indicated above);
- pre-trial document preparation;
- the trial hearing itself.

The listing questionnaire

The parties will be sent a listing questionnaire not more than eight weeks before the trial date or the beginning of the trial period (CPR 28.5(2)). The listing questionnaire (Form N170) asks the parties to answer the following questions:

- whether directions have been complied with and whether further directions are needed;
- whether the Court has given permission for experts, whether experts have met, whether the report is agreed, whether there are dates when the expert is unavailable;
- the number, names and addresses of any lay witnesses, the dates when they are available, whether their statements can be agreed, whether any special facilities are needed;
- whether a party is going to be legally represented and the dates when the legal representative is unavailable.

Upon receiving a properly completed listing questionnaire the court will confirm the date for trial (which should already have been set) and give any necessary directions for trial which may include specifying the place for trial (CPR 28.6 and Part 28, PD 7.1(1)). The Court will generally give the parties at least three weeks' notice of the confirmed date of trial unless (exceptionally) the Court directs that shorter notice will be given (CPR 28.6(2)).

A listing hearing will only be held by the Court in cases where a party fails to complete a listing questionnaire or if a listing questionnaire is inadequately completed (CPR 28.5(3)). The Practice Direction states that where no party files a listing questionnaire the Court will normally order that, unless a listing questionnaire is filed within three days, the claim and any counterclaim will be struck out (Part 28, PD 6.5(1)).

Postponing the trial

This matter is also discussed, in a slightly different context, in the *Fast Track Directions*, Chapter 5 above. It was a key feature of the automatic directions provisions of the old rules (CCR Ord 17, r 11) that a cardinal sin was the late adjournment (now known as "*postponement*") or vacation of a fixed trial date, particularly when this was necessitated by dilatory service of witness statements (see, *The Mortgage Corporation* v *Sandoes* [1997] PNLR 263 CA). This kind of thinking has been carried forward into the Rules. The Practice Direction provides:

> (1) The court will not allow a failure to comply with directions to lead to the postponement of the trial unless the circumstances are exceptional. (2) If it is practicable to do so the court will exercise its powers in a manner that enables the case to come on for trial on the date or within the period previously set. ... (5) Where the court has no option but to postpone the trial it will do so for the shortest possible time and will give directions for the taking of the necessary steps in the meantime as rapidly as possible.
>
> (Part 28, PD 5.4)

The same section of the Practice Direction also encourages the use of split trials and trial of preliminary issues as an alternative to the postponement of a trial (Part 28, PD 5.4(4)).

Pre-trial document preparation: trial bundles

The Rules provide that, unless the Court orders otherwise, the Claimant must have filed in advance a trial bundle containing all of the documents required by any relevant Practice Direction and any Court order (CPR 39.5(1)). The trial bundle must be filed not more than seven days and not less than three days before the start of the trial (CPR 39.5(2)). As a result of the constraints on the length of the fast track trial it will be necessary to give very careful thought to the documentation to be included in the trial bundle. The former minority practice of simply photocopying the entire file and paginating it should be avoided at all costs. The relevant Practice Direction gives guidance on what ought to go into the bundle:

- the claim form and all statements of case;
- requests for further information and responses thereto;
- all witness statement evidence;
- notice of intention to rely on hearsay evidence (under CPR 32.2);

- any notices of intention to rely on plans, photographs or other evidence (under CPR 33.6) which is not annexed to a witness statement, report or affidavit and which, not otherwise being given as live evidence, is hearsay;
- medical report(s) (usually just one report of a single joint expert);
- any further expert's reports (likely to be unusual in fast track claims);
- any order giving directions as to trial conduct;
- any other necessary documents (which should be scrupulously pared down to the relevant and necessary) (Part 39, PD 3.2).

The parties legal representatives should make the originals of the copy documentation available at Court, should paginate and index the trial bundle and where the pages exceed 100 should place dividers between the relevant sections. The bundle should be placed in a lever arch or ring binder and, where there is more than one of these, the two binders should be clearly distinguishable. It may be useful to prepare a *"core"* bundle. The parties should, where possible, agree the contents of the trial bundle. The party filing the bundle should make identical copies available to the other parties and to the court for the use of witnesses at trial.

In addition to the trial bundle the parties may well find it useful to prepare a costs bundle for argument as to the apportionment of costs at the conclusion of trial. It will certainly be necessary to prepare a costs schedule for exchange with the other party. These matters are dealt with in the *Costs* Chapter, Chapter 10 below.

The hearing

The Rules state that the trial will take place in accordance with any directions given previously unless the Judge directs otherwise (CPR 28.7). District Judges and Circuit Judges will enjoy concurrent jurisdiction in fast track matters in the County Court; it is envisaged that, eventually, District Judges will have sole jurisdiction over these matters.

The fast track trial must, of course, take place within the one day of Court time allotted to it which is defined as five hours of Court time (Part 26, PD 9.1(3)(a)). The Practice Direction states that the proceedings will be expedited by the fact that the Judge will "*generally*" have read the papers in advance and may dispense with an opening address (Part 28, PD 8.2). The Court is also empowered to limit the time allowed for cross-examination (CPR 32.1(3)) and will have to be prepared to make use of this power in order to ensure that the time-limit is complied with. The fact that served witness statements will stand as evidence-in-chief and that the Court will only allow supplement and addition to this evidence where there is a good reason for this will also move proceedings along (CPR 32.5(2)–(4)). It may be that the fast track trial timetable will look like this:

COMPONENT OF TRIAL	TIME ALLOWED
Opening address of Claimant (if any allowed)	10 minutes
Claimant's witness evidence (cross-examination and re-examination)	90 minutes
Defendant's witness evidence (cross-examination and re-examination)	90 minutes
Defendant's closing submissions	25 minutes
Claimant's closing submissions	25 minutes
Judge's consideration of evidence and judgment	30 minutes
Costs	30 minutes
TOTAL TIME	**5 HOURS**

This timetable is based on a number of assumptions. First, that the Judge will not need time to read the papers in advance on the day itself. Second, that the Judge does not dispense with an opening address. Third, that the parties do not ask for time (which may well be taken off the time table). Finally, and most importantly, that the case is able to be accommodated within the five hours allocated to it. The Practice Direction provides that, "*Where a trial is not finished on the day for which it is listed the judge will normally sit on the next court day to complete it.*" Of course, if this does happen the advocate who is successful will not be able to recover his refresher fee from the other side as a result of the fast track trial fixed costs regime (see, *Costs* chapter, Chapter 10 below). If the advocate is left out of pocket as a result of not finishing in one day and this is because of some inefficiency by the Court (for example, listing an emergency *ex parte/*"without notice" matter before a fast track Judge on the day fixed for trial) then it has been suggested that he may, perhaps, look to the Lord Chancellor's Department for compensation. Costs will ordinarily be summarily assessed, without the need for detailed assessment (formerly known as taxation), at the conclusion of the trial (Part 28, PD 8.5 for which, see, *Costs* chapter, Chapter 10 below).

The trial will ordinarily take place at the Court responsible for pre-trial case management unless Court resources and/or the needs of the parties make another location more suitable (Part 28, PD 8.1).

Costs

General features

The provision made by the Rules for the award of costs constitutes, perhaps, one of the most revolutionary aspects of the new regime. Six separate Parts of the Rules are dedicated to costs:

- Scope – Part 43;
- General Rules – Part 44;
- Fixed costs – Part 45;
- Fast Track trial costs – Part 46;
- Procedure for detailed assessment of costs and default provisions – Part 47;
- Costs (special cases) – Part 48.

Some of the key features of the new landscape with which legal practitioners must, perforce, be familiar are:

- the need to prepare a costs bundle and to be prepared to argue against the principle that the winning party is entitled to all (or even any) of its costs;
- the need to consider the reasonableness of costs before they are incurred and the proportionality of the costs claimed to the financial value of the claim;
- the duty to inform clients as to costs orders made at hearings that they do not attend (together with explanation of the reasons for the order);
- the preparation of a costs schedule to assist the summary assessment of the costs of an interim hearing lasting not more than one day and any trial hearing lasting not more than one day;
- the award of only fixed costs for advocates at a fast track trial.

These concepts are described and considered in more detail below.

The key principles and definitions

The general principle remains that the unsuccessful party will be required to pay the costs of the successful party (CPR 44.3(2)(a)). However, the Court retains a discretion to make a different Order (CPR 44.3(2)(b)) and, indeed, it is perhaps one of the most radical features of the new costs rules that the losing party will be positively encouraged, both by the Rules themselves and by the cultural change that they will engender, to raise arguments against the principle that winner takes all. The net result of this is that Court hearings in fast track cases are likely to be bedevilled by sometimes lengthy argument about the costs order that the Court should make in respect of the pre-trial conduct of an action. The parties' legal representatives at hearing will have to ensure that they are adequately armed with detailed information about the entire history of the action both before and after the commencement of proceedings. It will also be necessary to ensure that the conduct of the claim and the respective action and response of the parties is properly evidenced and easily digestible for the Judge charged with making the costs order. This is probably best done by preparation of a comprehensive and easy to follow costs bundle containing relevant correspondence and other documentation.

It should be borne in mind that the Rules provide that if the Court makes an order in which no mention is made of costs then neither party will be entitled to costs (CPR 44.13(1)).

As elsewhere the nomenclature has changed. A *"Costs Officer"* charged with the task of assessing costs is defined, *inter alia*, as a district judge or authorized court officer and an authorised court officer is, in turn, defined, *inter alia*, as any officer of the County Court. In addition, the party entitled to be paid costs becomes the *"receiving party"* and the party liable to pay them becomes the *"paying party"*. Taxation has become *"detailed assessment of costs"*.

A duty to inform the absent client

The Rules make special provision for information as to a costs order made by the Court to be passed on by a legal representative to his client. It is provided that where the Court makes a costs order against a legally represented party and the party is not present when the order is made then the party's solicitor must notify the party of the costs order not later than seven days after notice of the same is received by the solicitor (CPR 44.2). This provision is supplemented by the relevant Practice Direction which requires that, in order to comply with this duty, a solicitor must also explain why the order came to be made (Part 44, PD 1.2). Apparently, the original proposal was that a solicitor in default of the duty to inform would have to bear the liability for costs himself. This did not find its way into the final rule. It is suggested that the information provided by solicitor to client in the circumstances anticipated by this section of the Rules should always be put in writing so that it is readily available to the Court.

Fast track fixed costs

Insofar as fast track costs are concerned, the Lord Chancellor originally considered whether recoverable *inter partes* costs should be subject to a fixed maximum both pre-trial and at trial. Unsurprisingly, this suggestion did not meet with universal approval and the Rules, as implemented, make provision only for fixed costs at trial. The pre-trial costs of the parties will be assessed in accordance with the discretionary principles that are described below. It is possible that the solicitor's branch of the profession did a rather better job at lobbying for amendments to the proposals as originally conceived than did the junior Bar. There is, however, a potential sting in the tail in that a system for monitoring pre-trial fast track costs will be instituted after 26 April 1999 with a view to introducing a costs regime once sufficient information has been assembled.

Fast Track pre-trial costs: the Court's discretion as to costs

In relation to pre-trial costs the Court has, as stated above, a discretion as to:

- whether costs are payable by one party to the other;
- the amount of the costs; and
- when the costs are to be paid. (CPR 44.3(1)).

Discretion as to costs: the conduct of the parties

In respect of the Court's discretionary decision as to what costs order (if any) to make the Rules make detailed provision for the manner in which the discretion is to be exercised. A principal determinant is the *conduct* of all the parties (*ie.* not just the paying party) (CPR 44.3(4)(a)). The conduct of the parties is defined to include conduct during *and before* the proceedings and expressly requires that regard be had to the degree of compliance with the Pre-action Protocol (CPR 44.3(5)(a)). The draft Practice Direction on Protocols makes specific provision for regard to be had to the question whether non-compliance with the Pre-action Protocol has led to the commencement of proceedings that might not otherwise have been commenced. In these circumstances, the Court is empowered to order that the defaulting party pay all or part of the other party's costs of the proceedings on the indemnity basis (Protocols, draft PD 2.3(1)–(2)). If the defaulting party is a Claimant then he can be deprived of interest on his damages (Protocols, draft PD 2.3(3)). If the defaulting party is a Defendant then he can be ordered to pay interest on the sums awarded at a higher rate (not exceeding 10% above base rate) than he might otherwise have been ordered to pay (Protocols, draft PD 2.3(4)).

The court will also examine, *inter alia*, in regard to conduct, whether it was reasonable for a party to raise, pursue or contest a particular allegation or issue (CPR 44.3(5)(b)) and whether a claimant who has succeeded in whole or part has exaggerated his claim (CPR 44.3(5)(d)).

Discretion as to costs: Part 36 offers and payments

In addition to the conduct of all the parties, the Court is empowered, when deciding what costs order (if any) to make, to consider whether a party has succeeded on part of his claim, even if he has not been wholly successful (CPR 44.3 (4)(b)).

The Court will also have regard to any payment into court that has been made or any admissible offer to settle which is drawn to the attention of the Court (regardless of whether it was made formally in compliance with the terms of Part 36 of the Rules) (CPR 44.3(4)(c)).

Part 36 makes further detailed provision for the costs consequences of Part 36 payments-in and Claimant's offers to settle and Part 44 of the Rules specifically directs attention towards the same (CPR 44.3(4)). First, if a Part 36 Defendant's offer or payment-in is accepted by a Claimant without the need for permission from the Court then the Claimant will normally be entitled to costs on the standard basis of his claim (and any counterclaim if account is taken of the same in the offer or payment-in) up until the date of service of the notice of acceptance (CPR 36.13). The Court is vested with a discretion to order otherwise if the Defendant's offer or payment-in relates only to a part of the Claimant's claim and the latter indicates that it is taking the offer and abandoning the balance of the claim (CPR 36.13(2)). Similarly, where a Defendant accepts a Claimant's Part 36 offer to settle the Claimant will be entitled to costs up until the date of service of the notice of acceptance (CPR 36.14).

If the Claimant fails, at trial, to better a Part 36 offer or payment-in then the Court will ordinarily order the Claimant to pay any costs incurred by the Defendant after the latest date on which the offer or payment-in could have been accepted without needing the Court's permission (CPR 36.20). If the Defendant is held liable at trial for a greater sum than the proposals set out in the Claimant's offer to settle or if the judgment against the Defendant is more advantageous to the Claimant than the proposals previously made by the latter in an offer to settle, then the Defendant will face a punitive interest rate imposed on the sum awarded to the Claimant. The Rules provide that,

> The Court may order interest on the whole or part of any sum of money (excluding interest) awarded to the claimant at a rate not exceeding 10% above base rate for some or all of the period starting with the latest date on which the defendant could have accepted the offer without needing the permission of the court.
>
> (CPR 36.21(2)).

The Court can also compound the Defendant's misery by ordering that the Claimant is entitled to costs on the indemnity basis (and interest thereon at 10% above base rate) from the latest date when the Defendant could have accepted the offer to settle without needing the Court's permission (CPR 36.21(3)). Lest any District Judges be squeamish about imposing the penalties described above the Rules provide that the orders for punitive interest on damages and costs against the Defendant *will be made*, unless it is unjust to do so (CPR 36.21(4)). The Court is directed, *inter alia*, to the conduct of the parties, the terms of the offer to settle and the stage in the proceedings at which it was made in determining whether it would be unjust to penalize the Defendant in the manner that is described (CPR 36.21(5)).

Fast Track pre-trial costs: the range of costs orders available to the Court

The Court can order variously that a paying party is liable to pay:

- a proportion of another party's costs;
- a stated amount in respect of another party's costs;
- costs from or until a certain date only;
- costs incurred before proceedings have begun;
- costs relating to particular steps in the proceedings;
- costs relating only to distinct parts of the proceedings; and/or
- interest on costs from or until a certain date, including a date before judgment (CPR 44.3(6)).

There is (at least) one curious omission in the Rules in that there is no *express* provision made in the Rules for the solicitor's pre-trial costs in generally preparing for the fast track trial by taking witness statements and putting together a trial bundle. The assumption must be that these will be recoverable under the Court's general discretion as to costs in Part 44 (CPR 44.3).

Fast Track pre-trial costs: the standard and indemnity basis for the assessment of costs

The Court is empowered to assess costs on a standard or indemnity basis, but it will not allow in either case costs which have been unreasonably incurred or which are unreasonable in amount (CPR 44.4(1)). Where costs are allowed on a standard basis the Court will only allow those costs that are *proportionate* to the matters in issue between the parties (CPR 44.4(2)(a)). In standard assessment cases the Court simply will not allow those costs which have either been unreasonably incurred or which have been run up out of all proportion to the importance of the issues. The Courts will not allow the best to be the enemy of the good, parties are to be positively encouraged to moderate their spending and, where possible, to cut corners. It remains to be seen whether this will assist the efficient pre-trial preparation that will be necessary if a fast track case is to be effectively squeezed into the five hours of Court time allotted to it. It is the experience of this writer that if corners are cut pre-trial and if only a scrappy trial bundle is prepared the case will inevitably last longer at trial. In this regard it is worth bearing in mind the cautionary note sounded by the Practice Direction that supplements Part 44. It provides, *inter alia*,

> The relationship between the total of the costs incurred and the financial value of the claim may not be a reliable guide. A fixed percentage cannot be applied in all cases to the value of the claim in order to ascertain whether or not the costs are proportionate. .... in a modest claim the proportion of costs [relative to the amount of damages awarded] is likely to be higher than in a large claim, and may even equal or possibly exceed the amount in dispute. ... Where a trial takes place, the time taken by the court for dealing with a particular issue may not be an accurate guide to the amount of time properly spent by the legal or other representatives in preparation for the trial of that issue.

(Part 44, PD 3.1–3.3).

Clearly, this Practice Direction provision offers some crumbs of comfort to practitioners with a large fast track case load and may well become one of the most regularly cited and invoked passages in the costs Part of the Rules.

As under the old rules, standard assessment places a burden on *the receiving party* to prove that the costs were reasonably incurred and proportionate (CPR 44.4(2)(b)). The burden of proving that the costs were unreasonably incurred by the receiving party is placed on *the paying party* where the same are assessed on the indemnity basis (CPR 44.4(3)). In assessing the reasonableness or otherwise and, for standard costs, the proportionality of costs the Court will have regard to:

- the conduct of the parties before and after the commencement of proceedings;
- any efforts to resolve the dispute;

- the amount or value of any money involved;
- the importance of the matter to the parties;
- the complexity of the issues in dispute;
- the skill, effort and specialized knowledge involved;
- the place where and circumstances in which the work or part of it was done.

This criteria for assessment are ranked in order of importance. It is significant that the importance of an issue to the parties is ranked somewhere down the priority list: will this deter all those litigants for whom their dispute is or becomes "*a matter of the highest principle*"? It is also important to note that the time spent on the case is ranked second to last in the list. It is difficult to be optimistic that this will result in more efficient use of time, rather than in rushed preparation.

Fast Track trial costs: the method of assessment

Part 44 of the Rules (CPR 44.9) directs attention to Part 46 of the Rules in which special provision is made in respect of liability for costs, the amount of costs to be paid and the procedure by which costs are to be assessed. The special rules in Part 46 do not apply until a case is allocated to the fast track (CPR 44.9(2)). If a case allocated to the fast track settles before the date fixed for trial the Court cannot make a costs order in respect of the advocate's costs that exceeds the fixed amount that would have been recoverable had the trial actually taken place (CPR 44.10(1)). In considering the advocate's costs in such a situation the court is also directed by the Rules to have regard to when the case settled and to when the court was notified that the case had settled (CPR 44.10(2)). If a case is allocated to the fast track and is re-allocated to a different track by the Court before trial the Court will apply the fast track costs regime up until the date of re-allocation (CPR 44.11(2)).

Part 46 which applies to the costs of an advocate preparing for and appearing at a trial in a fast track claim defines the "*advocate*" as, "*a person exercising a right of audience as a representative of, or on behalf of, a party*" and further defines "*fast track trial costs*" as, "*the costs of a party's advocate for preparing for and appearing at the trial*", which does not include any other disbursements or any value added tax payable on the advocate's fees (CPR 46.1(2)). It should be noted that the fast track trial costs regime described in detail below does not apply to disposal hearings (formerly known as assessment of damages hearings). This is regardless of the financial value of the claim. The costs of a disposal hearing remain in the discretion of the court. (CPR 46.1(c), Part 46, PD 1.3(b) and Part 26, PD 12.9(4)).

The fast track trial costs are fixed, whether they are summarily assessed or assessed in detail, and the amount recoverable is pegged to the financial value of the claim. Where the Claimant's costs are awarded the financial value of the claim is calculated by reference to the judgment sum by excluding interest, costs and any reduction for contributory negligence (CPR 46.2(3)(a)). Where the Defendant's costs are awarded, financial value is based on the amount specified in the claim form (excluding costs and interest) or, if no sum is specified, the statement of value in the claim form is used (CPR 46.2(3)(b)). If the Claimant states that he cannot reasonably state how much he expects to recover he will be penalized by the Rules which will assess the Defendant's fast track trial costs by assuming that the financial value of the Claimant's claim exceeds £10,000 (CPR 46.2(3)(b)(iii)). Clearly, it will be in the Claimant's interests to give as accurate as possible an estimate of financial value. The failure to given any indication as to financial value should be avoided if at all possible. In cases where a Defendant counterclaims and the same has a higher financial value than the claim and the Claimant succeeds at trial on claim and counterclaim the value of the Defendant's counterclaim will be adopted to fix the costs recoverable by the Claimant at trial (CPR 46.2(6)). If the Claimant and the Defendant both succeed on claim and counterclaim respectively, the Court will quantify the award of fast track trial costs to which, but for the counterclaim the Claimant would be entitled, and to which, but for the claim the Defendant would be entitled, and will make one award, calculated as the difference between the two, to the party entitled to the higher award of costs (CPR 46.3(6)).

Fast Track trial costs: the fixed sums

The following table appears in Part 46 and sets the fixed costs that are recoverable at trial according to the method of assessment described above (CPR 46.2(1)).

VALUE OF CLAIM	AMOUNT OF FAST TRACK TRIAL COSTS THAT THE COURT MAY AWARD
Up to £3,000	£350
More than £3,000 but not more than £10,000	£500
More than £10,000	£750

There are very limited circumstances in which the Court may disapply the fixed costs set out above, whether by awarding more or less than the sums prescribed (CPR 46.2(2)). If the court considers that it was necessary for a party's legal representative to attend court in addition to the advocate and that party is awarded fast track trial costs then a further £250 may be awarded in trial costs (CPR 46.3(2)). If the court considers it necessary to direct a separate trial of a specific issue then it may award costs that do not exceed two-thirds of the amount payable as fixed costs under the table above, subject to a minimum additional sum of £350 (CPR 46.3(3)–(4)). Where a party appears in person at trial the court will award a litigant able to prove financial loss occasioned by attendance at trial a sum equal to two-thirds of what would be awarded for an advocate under the table above. The court is also empowered to vary upwards or downwards the sum awarded as fixed costs where the paying or receiving party has acted unreasonably or improperly during the trial (CPR 46.3(7)–(8)).

There is further specific provision in the Rules for the situation in which there is more than one Claimant or Defendant. If the same advocate acts for more than one party the Court can refuse to make more than one costs award (CPR 46.4(1)). If the same advocate acts for more than one Claimant and each Claimant pursues a separate claim against the Defendant the value of the claim for the purposes of calculating fast track trial costs is the total financial value of the judgment made in favour of all the Claimants jointly represented or, where the Defendant is successful, of the total amount claimed by the Claimants (CPR 46.4(3)). If there is more than one Defendant and any or all of the Defendants are separately represented the Court is empowered to award fast track trial costs to each separately represented Defendant (CPR 46.4(4)).

The procedure for assessing costs

Costs are either assessed summarily or in detail (CPR 44.7). The Rules make provision for summary assessment in fast track cases and the Courts will be actively encouraged to make use of this power. The Practice Direction makes it clear that the Court should generally make a costs order at the end of a fast track trial in respect of the costs of the whole action (Part 44, PD 4.4(1)(a)). Similarly, the Court should generally embark on a summary assessment of the costs of an interlocutory application where that application was heard in less than one day (Part 44, PD 4.4(1)(b)). The Court will not be able to assess the costs summarily where the costs of the application are awarded as costs "*in the case*" (formerly, costs in cause) (Part 44, PD 4.4(2)). The Courts are, therefore, to be discouraged from awarding costs in the case. Where the parties agree an interim order by consent and without the need for their attendance they should make provision for the costs of that application or agree that there should be no order as to costs (Part 44, PD 4.4(3)).

A key aspect of summary assessment which will be the norm for all fast track cases is the need for the parties to prepare a schedule of costs setting out:

- the number of hours claimed;
- the hourly rate to be claimed;
- the grade of the fee earner;
- the amount and nature of any disbursement claimed, other than counsel's fee at the hearing;
- the solicitor's costs for attendance at the hearing;
- the value added tax claimed (Part 44, PD 4.5(2)).

The schedule must be signed by a party or by his legal representative and must be filed at Court and exchanged with the other party not less than 24 hours before the hearing (Part 44, PD 4.5(4)). The failure of any party, without reasonable excuse, to comply with the provisions as to preparation and service of the costs schedule will be taken into account by the Court when assessing costs and will, no doubt, be used in a punitive fashion against the defaulting party (Part 44, PD 4.6). The Court will award a single sum on summary assessment that will comprise all sums allowed inclusive of profit costs, disbursements and value added tax and the fast track trial costs (Part 44, PD 4.7). Summary assessment will not apply to cases where the receiving party is legally aided or is a child or patient bringing proceedings through a litigation friend (Part 44, PD 4.9). The parties can also agree their costs which will obviate the need for summary assessment and costs schedules (Part 44, PD 4.10).

The Rules on detailed assessment of costs are set out in Part 47 of the Rules and the Practice Direction that supplements the same. They incorporate principles that will be fairly familiar to those who attended taxation hearings under the old rules. As detailed assessment will generally be irrelevant to fast track cases it is not proposed to examine these rules. Legal aid cases will continue to be subject to detailed assessment and will be assessed in a similar fashion to legal aid taxation under the old rules. However, the basis of assessment will be the *standard* basis and, thus, the principle of proportionality will be applied to cut the sums paid by the Legal Aid Board to solicitors.

The assessment of conditional fee arrangements

The basic cost, disregarding the uplift, will be assessed on the indemnity basis as with all solicitor and own client costs. However, the conditional uplift will also be subject to assessment and can, therefore, be reduced as unreasonable (Part 48, PD 2.13(1)). In assessing the reasonableness or otherwise of the uplift the Rules direct the Court to have regard, *inter alia*, to the risks of not being paid at all that are faced by lawyers taking cases on the basis of a conditional fee agreement (Part 48, PD 2.15). The Court is directed to have regard to the risks faced by the lawyer *at the time that the conditional fee agreement is entered into;* the risk cannot, with hindsight, be underestimated by the Court as a justification for reducing the uplift (Part 48, PD 2.13(2) and 2.16).

Wasted costs

It is not proposed to set out the provision made by the Rules for wasted costs orders which differs little from the position under the old rules (CPR 48.7).

Index

Access to Justice, 1, 3–7
Acknowledgement of claim, 11
Advocates' costs, 51
Affidavit, 36, 37
Alternative Dispute Resolution, 22
Allocation, 20–23, 25
Allocation questionnaire, 20–21, 23
Anton Piller, *see* Search order
APIL, 6–7
Applications, 30–31
Assessors, 40
Automatic directions, 2
Automatic stays, 9

Case management, x, 4–5, 20
Claim form, 15–17
Claimant's offer to settle, 41
Commencing proceedings, 13–17
Compensation Recovery, 42
Conditional fee arrangements,
    assessment of, 62–63
Cost-effectiveness, ix, 4
Costs, 10, 41, 51–63
    Assessment of, 58–59, 61–62
    Conduct of the parties and, 54
    Costs bundle, need for, 51
    Costs schedule, 51
    Court's discretion, 53–56
    Detailed assessment of, 52
    Fixed costs, 51, 53, 59, 60–61
    Informing clients, 51, 52–53
    Offers and payments, 54–56
    Pre-trial costs, 56–58
    Principles, 52

Proportionality and, 56–58
Reasonableness, 51
Sanctions, 28
Wasted costs, 63
Court of Appeal, ix, 1–2

Directions for the fast track, 26–29
    Failure to comply, 28–29
    Varying, 28
Disclosure, 24, 25–26, 27

Efficiency, x, 4
Equality, ix, 4
Evidence, 36–40
Exchange of witness statements, 26
Expert evidence, 24, 26, 27, 36–40
    Exchange of reports, 27
    Form of report, 39–40
    Trial bundle and, 48

Fast track
    Allocation to, 20–23
    Applications, 30–35
    Costs, 51–63
    Definition, 5, 6, 8–10
    Directions, 26–29
    Evidence, 36–40
    Offers, 41–44
    Summary disposal, 30–35
    Summary judgement, 30–35
    Trials, 45–50
Freezing injunction, 32
Further information, 19, 26, 27, 31

Guardian ad litem, *see* Litigation friend

Inspection of documents, 26
Interest on judgment debt, 41
Interim payments, 32–33
Interim remedies, 31–32
Interlocutory remedies *see* Interim remedies

Judges, role of, ix, 4–5

Letter of claim, 11
Letter of reply, 12
Listing questionnaire, 27, 45, 46
Litigation friend, 14

Mareva injunction *see* Freezing injunction

Offeree, 41
Offeror, 41
Offers to settle, 41–44
    Time limits on, 43
Overriding objective, ix, x, 4

Particulars of claim, 15–17
    Defence and, 17–18
Parties, 14–15
    Adding or substituting a, 31
Payments into court, 41–44
Pleadings, *see* Statements of case
Pre-action protocols, 8, 10, 11–13
Procedural flexibility, 1–3
Proportionality, ix, 4, 6
    Costs and, 56–58
    Inspection and, 26
Provisional damages, 42

Replies, directions for, 26

Search order, 32
Service of witness statements, 24, 26
Single joint expert, 26, 39
Standard disclosure, *see* Disclosure
Statements of case, 13–14, 18
    Abusive, 34
    Amendments to, 26, 31
Statements of truth, 13–14, 37
Stays of proceedings, 22
Striking out, *see* Summary disposal
Summary disposal, 30, 31, 32, 33–34
Summary judgment, 30, 31, 32, 33, 34–35

Taxation, *see* Costs, detailed assessment of
Third party claims, 19
Tracks, 4–5
Transitional arrangements, 8–9
Trial, 45–50
    Hearing, 48–50
    Listing, 46
    Postponing, 46–47
    Pre-trial documentation, 47–48
    Timetable for, 49
Trial bundle, 47–48

Unless orders, 33

Wasted costs, 63
Witness statements,
    Exchange of, 27
    Form of, 37–38
    Service of, 24
    Use of, 36–37